Growing Community

Making groups work with
young people

DANNY BRIERLEY

LIFESTYLE

OAS!S
youth action

Authentic Lifestyle is an imprint of
Authentic Media, PO Box 300, Kingstown Broadway
Carlisle, Cumbria CA3 0QS, UK
and Box 1047, Waynesboro, GA 30830-2047, USA
www.paternoster-publishing.com

British Library Cataloguing in Publication Data

A catalogue record for this book is available from the British
Library

ISBN 1-85078-484-1

Cover design by Sam Redwood
Printed in Great Britain by
Cox and Wyman Ltd., Reading

To Sally, Millie and Jasmine

Contents

Part 3: Resourcing Groups

Preface

Over the years, I have had the privilege of serving on the staff of two very dynamic, yet different, churches: Chawn Hill Christian Centre, Stourbridge and Altrincham Baptist Church in Greater Manchester. Regrettably not all youth workers are able to speak so highly of their churches. I owe a huge debt to all the volunteers and staff I have worked with over the years. This book reflects our shared experiences. Particular mention is due to Sally Walker-Smith, Dave Clarke and Steve Cockram.

Now I have the privilege of working with a very creative and committed team of people at Oasis Trust and am grateful for all their encouragement and support. In addition, as part of *Youthwork – the Partnership* I appreciate my involvement with Richard Bromley (YFC), John Buckeridge (*Youthwork Magazine*), Jim Partridge (Spring Harvest) and Russell Rook (Salvation Army).

This book is an updated and expanded version of *Young People and Small Groups* (Scripture Union, 1997). I am grateful to Laura Hughes for all her work on the manuscript. Since 1997 there has been renewed interest in group work, helped in large part by the cell-church

movement. Throughout the book I have deliberately
referred to both small and cell groups. It is important to
distinguish between the two and yet many group work
principles are common to both. I hope those with a general interest in group work will find this book a helpful
introduction to cell-church principles, and that those
already committed to 'cells' will gain useful insights into
making groups work.

Other people's ministries often sound far more effective than our own, and I urge you not to take everything
I say at face value. All youth work and ministry is a
struggle at times. But team effort can play an enormous
part in the development of good ideas and working
practice. I hope you will find that this book challenges,
and goes some way towards equipping, you to serve the
needs of the young people in your local community.

Danny Brierley, 2003

Part 1

DEVELOPING GROUPS

1

Small groups, big need

The minibus stopped and six people leapt out into the unknown. Ahead lay four gruelling days of walking, navigating and problem-solving.

We had started the Outward Bound course as six individuals, each with something to prove[1]. I was fifteen years old and the youngest member of the group, new to outdoor pursuits and not very fit. Darren was a soldier in the Cheshire Regiment, who relished every opportunity of doing unto others what had, in the army, been done unto him. David, the joker of the pack, was making a career out of being a trainee civil engineer; while Paul, a computer programmer, was quiet and very capable. Typically last was Stuart, a student who lived in the shadow of his Falklands War hero father. As diverse as we were, we had just three weeks to change ourselves into a cohesive and functioning small group.

We argued bitterly, worked hard, laughed, occasionally failed and, as a result, became friends. Common experience and time spent together enabled us to overcome our differences. We finished the course feeling that, as a group, there wasn't much we couldn't do.

After the course, I returned to school and did what my zealous youth leader had been urging me to do for some time: I 'came out'! During a wet break, with much apprehension, I announced to my class that I had become a Christian – actually, some eighteen months earlier. There was now no turning back.

What was it that had made my declaration possible? It was, I believe, the demanding small group experience I had gone through on the course. It enabled me to discover a new level of self-confidence, making it easier for me to stick up for my beliefs. After all, the challenge of the classroom was not that dissimilar to the challenge I faced on the mountainside: both required determination, occasional discomfort and a desire to succeed.

Now imagine what the impact would be if the young people in your youth ministry were able to experience the kind of support and empowerment I received during that expedition in Scotland. It is my belief that developing a ministry built on small or cell groups can make this possible.

Small or cell groups work in organisations of any size. They enable modestly sized youth ministries to grow numerically, and big youth ministries to grow relationally. Six people can form one small or cell group; sixty can form up to ten groups. The principles by which each group operates will be the same, and the potential for further growth will be equal. I will outline in Chapter 3 the types of groups that are available to youth workers. Throughout the book I will use 'small-group ministries' to refer to those that are intentionally built on small groups. A group that happens to comprise few members would qualify as a small-group ministry if the intention is to meet future growth by forming new small groups. However, it would not qualify as a 'small-group ministry' if future growth would simply result in a bigger group.

Small or cell groups come in a range of shapes and sizes, but they all have one thing in common: they seek to provide an intimate environment where people are treated as individuals, not just members of a crowd. Each young person knows, and is known by, a handful of peers and a designated leader. By taking part in a range of social as well as spiritual pursuits, group members can be helped to discover and make the most of their gifts and abilities, perhaps even developing new leadership skills. Meanwhile, youth leaders have the opportunity to establish better links with a greater number of young people. In short, small or cell groups work.

But can this strong sense of community and personal identity only be achieved through small or cell groups? Surely it should be a natural part of youth ministry anyway?

Why small or cell groups?

The world young people inhabit is constantly changing. Charles Handy, business guru and committed Christian, describes this as being an 'age of unreason' dominated by 'discontinuous change'.[2] By this, he means that we are experiencing not the gradual improvement of the *status quo*, nor even 'more of the same only better', but rather dramatic and unpredictable change caused, among other things, by sudden shifts in thinking, catastrophic events or new inventions. Who, for example, could have predicted the dramatic impact that Alexander Bell's telephone has had, or the effect that satellite technology is having on global communication? Young people must make sense of this age at a time when they are at their most vulnerable, physically and emotionally. Let's look more closely at some of the changes and explore how the support of small or cell groups might help young people to adapt.

Community meltdown

Ever since Adam discovered Eve, human beings have striven for meaningful relationships. Young people, like adults, long for authentic community, and yet advances in society may actually stand in the way of their achieving this. (A more detailed explanation of 'community' can be found in Chapter 9.)

Technological revolution

Advanced technology is making both positive and negative contributions to young people's sense of community. To be invited into a teenager's bedroom (a privilege indeed) is to enter another domain. The teenage world is one of home computers, bedroom videos, dial-a-pizzas and the Internet. Surfing, megabytes, chips, webs and DVDs are everyday currency to this techno-friendly generation.[3]

New technology is not, in itself, negative. Young people are harnessing technology to create new forms of community that up to now have been impossible. One girl I worked with met her boyfriend in cyberspace. She lived in south Manchester, he in south Australia. After some time telecommuting via the Internet, they finally met face-to-face. An almost unlimited number of friendships are possible courtesy of these invisible electronic meeting-places. Such friendships may not develop in the traditional way but, by bringing people together, they can foster community. Six young people I worked with formed a small group with each of them attending different universities. They met face-to-face during the vacations, but for the rest of the time used e-mail and the Internet to communicate. The group also provided a virtual Agony Aunt/Uncle service for the young people back at home – a demonstration of how new technology can be used to further community and commitment to others.

New technology is, however, also having a negative impact on young people's sense of community. Whether as a result of television or computer-related activities, many young people appear to be spending increasing amounts of time in self-imposed isolation. Why else, when you live no more than a few minutes walk from your friends, would you choose to talk to them (for hours!) on the telephone?

Small or cell groups bring young people together, providing an environment in which they can meet regularly face-to-face. There is something refreshing about a group of young people who choose to spend time with each other, bonded by a common purpose. I will never forget hearing a parent, who had once urged her daughter to be involved in the youth ministry, complain that she was now spending too much time with her small group. Youth workers, be cautious when parents speak well of you!

Social revolution

Changes in society are gradually reducing the sense people once had of having 'roots' in a particular place. Increasing mobility means that many young people frequently have to leave behind established friendships when they move to different parts of the country and start again. For some, this becomes a pattern of life, with the result that they have fewer but more intense friendships.

Increasing demands in the workplace often mean that parents have less time to give than young people need. 'Quality time' has replaced 'quantity time'. The extended family living in close proximity is becoming a thing of the past.

With the family having less influence, many young people seek support from their peers. Christian sociologist Tony Campolo attributes the current rise in gang culture to their search for authentic community.[4] Gangs, which were once synonymous with inner-city disadvantaged groups, are now as likely to consist of suburban, advantaged young people. The make and cut of clothing, the type of footwear, the hair styles, all help to identify individuals as members of a gang. In turn, gang membership offers a sense of belonging and a set of rules to live by, even if those rules are different to those generally accepted by mainstream society. Campolo concludes that gangs provide young people with the sense of community that the church often talks about but seldom provides.

Small or cell groups can enable young people to develop genuine friendships and create authentic communities. Some small-group ministries, like that adopted by Willow Creek's Student Impact, encourage an element of competition between their groups as a means of encouraging the 'rebel' within each person. The feeling that it's 'us against the world' enhances the group's sense of belonging. Each young person is then able to affirm 'I know who I belong to and what is involved'.

Violent revolution

Contrary to popular belief, crime in Britain is at its lowest for more than twenty years. Yet, fear of violent crime is also having a negative impact on community. Many young people, who would once have spent time in public places with their peers, are now kept under constant supervision and told 'not to talk to strangers'. Many parents, understandably, try to ensure that their children are delivered to, and collected from, various activities. 'Strangers' are now not even assumed to be adult males. High-profile crimes committed by young people against young people exacerbate the popular belief that young people are simultaneously at risk from and a danger to others. A well-organised small or cell groups ministry will help to reassure parents of their young people's safety – they know who the young people are with, what they are doing and where. And Christian-based youth ministry offers community-deficient young people something worth belonging to.

The cumulative effect of the social changes mentioned above is the gradual erosion of community life. While small or cell groups may not be the only means of developing community, they do seem to be effective.

Communication meltdown

Parents know only too well the code of silence among young people that forbids them to answer questions such as 'Did you have a nice day, dear?' in words of more than one syllable. After all, who hasn't watched *Kevin and Perry*? But is it fair to say that communication skills are less developed in young people now than they once were?

Young people have always been good at evolving their own language. I well remember the craze at school for CB radios and the bizarre 'handles', or nicknames, we used to identify ourselves. Mine was Boney

Maroney! Now the techno-speak of computers and the Internet have taken over, but the basic principle remains the same: those 'in the know' use coded language to include peers while excluding the rest. By so doing, they intentionally, or otherwise, create a sense of belonging and identity. Nothing is guaranteed to speed the evolution of young people's language faster than the attempt by adult outsiders to adopt it as their own. So while not all young people are competent at speaking BBC English, it is probably fair to say that most are adept at communicating in their own way.

Communication, however, involves more than words. The skill of establishing relationships is one that young people can only learn from others. The increasingly vulnerable state of family life may be denying them suitable role models. Young people may not be able to resolve conflict because they have not seen conflict resolved by those closest to them. Tragically, it seems bad habits are passed from one generation to another. But if the institution of lifelong partnership is to survive as the primary expression of family, today's young people will need to develop communication skills greater than those of their parents. How might they do this?

Baz had worked hard at developing his 'bad boy' reputation. He came from a chaotic family background, had been permanently excluded from school and was no stranger to the courts. But Baz secretly wanted to change. He just didn't know how. After we'd had a few conversations, I suggested that we create a 'Waffle Group'[5] for him and his select entourage, in which they could talk through a range of issues. Baz agreed, so his mates joined in too!

Every week they would start walking up the hill to my house together, but by the time they had got half way they would have fallen out. Their arguments were fierce and sometimes violent, often caused by seemingly trivial matters; someone drinking half the can when he had only been offered a sip, or not waiting for someone else at the agreed place. They simply didn't know how to resolve conflict without resorting to brute strength. However, as this wasn't allowed in the Waffle Group, it became a safe haven for them all. We would focus on a pressing issue that was affecting them, and begin to talk it through, making sure we included a brief look at what the Bible had to say. On one occasion, 'Do not let the sun go down while you are still angry' became 'Do not let the shop close without first getting things sorted'. These lively sessions, though demanding, were extremely rewarding to lead.

Though the Waffle Group officially met only once a week, we used to have other informal gatherings far more frequently than that, usually around 4pm under a particular railway bridge. Without these extra meetings, there would not have been sufficient trust and rapport to make the small group work. Because the Waffle Group was small, there was no room to hide and, for it to survive, the members had to learn to relate well to each other. Not everyone did. In a large group, it is possible to ignore relationship difficulties – 'ignorance is bliss' – but in a small group it is not. You don't need to be a genius to recognise when two of the five young people in your group have fallen out! However, most relational difficulties can be resolved with careful handling if there is commitment to the small group. For some young people, the resolution of conflict may be a new experience.

The flexibility of small or cell groups means that they can work in any socio-economic environment. In Stourbridge, in England's West Midlands, the Waffle Group catered for a subculture of young people who appeared to have opted out of mainstream society. Later, in Altrincham, I served some of the most advantaged young people in the country.

Participation meltdown

'Meaningless! Meaningless! ... Utterly meaningless! Everything is meaningless' (Ecc. 1:2) has become the anthem of those unflatteringly identified as 'Millennial Kids'. Parents and youth workers often complain that they are an apathetic age group, unappreciative of anything provided for them. In our consumer society, marketing companies pay close attention to the needs and desires of young people (though this attention tends to last for as long as they continue to buy the right products!). Some companies co-opt representative young people into their power structures to enable product developers and advertisers to understand their market better. It is not hard to see how some young people may come to feel exploited.

The same is true of politics. Surveys reveal that only a minority of young people believe it matters which political party is in government. Just 19 per cent claim belief that party politics matter, with a further 32 per cent unsure.[6] Not surprising perhaps when they remain disenfranchised until they are eighteen years old. Many, it appears, have become disillusioned with mainstream politics and, in particular, with politicians who appear to put self-interest above the interests of those they purport to serve.

Because they want to be heard, a few young people turn to special interest groups and direct action campaigns. Dedicated eco-warriors campaign against potentially damaging new transport schemes by heading, not for the public inquiries but, for the trees and tunnels, where their views will be listened to more attentively. For others, even direct action seems ultimately futile – the 'system' always wins. Better, therefore, to head for the beach. In between the eco-warriors and the fun-seekers stand the majority, not motivated enough to live in trees or tunnels, but not cynical enough to opt out altogether. Somebody should probably do something, but not them. Sure, they will sign the petition if someone else will organise it.

Many young people feel equally disenfranchised by the church. Too many congregations still communicate, possibly quite unintentionally, the message that young people should be seen but rarely heard. On both occasions that I was appointed to a church staff young people were not, in reality, involved in the process. I was invited to observe a couple of youth group sessions, but the young people themselves had little opportunity to voice their own opinion as to whether or not they felt I was suitable for the job. The interviews and final decision involved only the adults in the church. Even youth groups can appear to value young people's attendance more than their participation. A diet of games, trips and meaningful thoughts is fine if you 'buy in' to the programme. If you don't, often the only way to register an opinion is to opt out, which helps neither the young person nor the youth worker responsible for the group.

Elspeth is great, but there was a time when I considered her both troublesome and disruptive. The simple reality was, she was bored by the youth programme. She had no say in what she did, felt unable to ask the questions that mattered to her, and was not challenged by the trivial games and the 'God-slots'. Her disruptive behaviour was, I now recognise, the only way she could signal her frustration. Ultimately, it was I who was at fault.

A few months later, we had a residential weekend, which was run entirely in small or cell groups of approximately four to six young people and an adult. Instead of listening to lectures and being told what the games were going to be, Elspeth and the others sat around and chewed over a range of issues. They could choose to agree or disagree; they could change the direction of the discussions; they could challenge simplistic statements. We all knew we had experienced something quite different, and we liked it. And Elspeth was changed by the experience. She became one of the most dedicated and supportive of the young people in the group, and eventually led a small group of her own. Her small group provided an environment in which she could speak, knowing she would be heard. She could ask awkward questions expecting that she would get an honest response. Through this she also learnt to handle responsibility.

A small group helps to build up each individual member. Each person must take into account the specific needs, views and talents of the others, because to ignore just one person would be to ignore, say, 20 per cent of the entire group. No organisation could ever do that and hope to survive. In a safe and encouraging environment, young people can feel free to express themselves and to discover their abilities. The role of the small-group leader should never be to *do* youth work *to* young people. Rather, they must enable each individual to become a more complete person; physically, intellectually, socially, emotionally and spiritually. My experience is that, generally, few young people remain apathetic when they are given the encouragement and the opportunity to participate in something they can believe in.

Meanwhile ...

On a mountain in Scotland, I and the small group of people with whom I was thrown together wrestled with the real issues of temperament, ability and personal values. Yes, it was demanding. Yes, it was frustrating. And yes, it was humbling. But, as a result, we emerged changed people. We had each achieved things we never thought we could, and each left with a higher regard for the contribution of others. Is this what you want for your young people? I believe that developing an intentional small-group ministry could radically transform your youth work.

Nevertheless, before getting too excited we need to consider whether small or cell groups have a biblical mandate. If they don't, we should be courageous enough to end our journey here. However, before doing that, it's homework time.

Homework

- If you haven't already done so, update the list of young people who are currently connected with your youth ministry, including their names, addresses, telephone numbers and dates of birth. Try to establish a regular attendance register.

- For one month keep a log of how much contact, both in and outside formal youth group sessions, these young people have with you or another youth worker. If the formal youth group sessions were to end suddenly, would the contact with each young person be maintained?

- Informally interview one or two young people who, for whatever reason, have stopped attending the youth programme, and ask them why.

2

Small groups, big example

I'm a believer in the Kingdom,
I am a seeker of the new things,
I am a dreamer with some old dreams.
Let them now come.
(Matt Redman, *Soul Survivor Music, 1997*)

In an innovative and forward-thinking generation, it remains no less necessary for us to look back. In seeking to develop a small or cell group ministry, we must first turn to the Bible. Not only does it contain timeless truths, it also describes unique events requiring specific responses. What worked two thousand years ago may not be appropriate today. We will therefore be seeking to draw out biblical principles rather than focusing on detail. And, as the Bible can only be fully understood in the light of the example and teaching of Christ, it is to the Gospels that we first look for our mandate.

Jesus

Almost as soon as Jesus began his public ministry, large crowds of people began to follow him. But Jesus would often withdraw from them, and go off to be alone or with his disciples (Mt. 5:1, 2). He wasn't being reclusive; rather, he was establishing an important principle that we would do well to learn.

Jesus sought to turn the world upside down, not by working the crowds but, by concentrating on a small number of individuals who would stay with him, learn from him and actively participate in pioneering his ministry (Mk. 3:14). In doing so, he became the supreme example of a small-group leader. Tearfund's motto of changing the world one life at a time seems to sum up Jesus' approach. Those few followers would, with his encouragement and inspiration, eventually become the largest religious movement in the world. Every Christian today can trace their spiritual heritage back to that one small group. If you consider your youth ministry to be small, then take encouragement from the example Jesus gives, and expect the unexpected!

In a busy world, it can be tempting for youth workers to timetable everything. But Jesus' small group had a life beyond the formal sessions. They spent considerable time together discussing, arguing, travelling, worshipping, eating and living. The disciples learnt about prayer through Jesus' example; they learnt about justice by watching him give dignity and value to the oppressed. These times together were not supplementary to the process, they were the process. Jesus, as the small-group leader, did not deliver a programme or control an agenda. Rather, he used the disciples' questions and everyday situations – a walk through a field, a sailing trip or a visit to the temple – as vehicles for drawing out his learning points. This was informal education *par excellence*. I have written more extensively about this in *Joined Up: An introduction to youth work and ministry* (Authentic, 2003).

Jewish and Greek culture both placed great significance on the teacher-disciple relationship.[7] Rabbis would sit on a low platform surrounded by their hand-picked disciples (or learners) who would seek to follow not only their rabbi's teaching but also his lifestyle. In turn, these disciples became teachers themselves, with their own band of disciples who would continue to copy their teaching and lifestyle. Jesus appears to have continued this tradition, but with one difference: though his twelve followers are described as being 'disciples' 225 times in the Gospels, Jesus himself is recorded as using the term only twice (Jn. 13:35; 15:8), preferring instead to call them 'brothers' (Mt. 12:49; 28:10), 'children' (Mk. 10:24; Jn. 13:33) and 'friends' (Lk. 12:4; Jn. 15:15). Jesus' small group was very inclusive and community-centred.

The disciples were small-group members, but there would come a time when, following the teacher-disciple pattern, they would establish new small or cell groups all over the region, replicating what they themselves had experienced.

While he was still grieving over his cousin John's brutal murder, Jesus attempted to withdraw to a place away from the crowds and the demands made on him. Nevertheless, the multitudes came looking for him (Mt. 14:13–21; Mk. 6:30–44; Lk. 9:10–17; Jn. 6:1–13) and, seeing them, compassionately set about ministering to them and healing the sick. This must have taken some time for, we are told, the disciples became anxious that the people would be hungry because they hadn't eaten all day. They wanted to send them all away to find food. Jesus' response must have stunned them: 'You give them something to eat.' This was no small challenge. How, in such a remote place, were twelve ordinary people going to feed five thousand men, not to mention the women and children? The disciples were at a loss; they had barely enough to feed themselves.

In Jesus' hands, five loaves and two fish became a meal for thousands. He made supernatural provision but, logistically, the disciples were unable to distribute the benefits on their own. So, he directed them to organise the people into smaller groups (Mk. 6:40) and, as a result, everyone received what they needed.

Most youth workers it seems – whether they are full-time or volunteers – find it struggle enough to care for their own young people, let alone the thousands of others who live in their area. Where I live there are approximately six thousand young people of which probably ninety per cent have no real spiritual sustenance. Jesus says to me and my co-workers, 'You give them something to eat.'

What would happen to our youth ministries if we surrendered to Christ what little we had, and asked him to use it to serve the needs of the wider community? Most youth workers limit the size of their mission field because they simply cannot comprehend taking on anything extra. One more appointment, one more meeting, they believe, and it's 'Goodnight, Reality.' As a result, they risk becoming bottlenecks, restricting what God is able to do in their communities. But what if ministry were a shared task?

Interestingly, only John records that the loaves and fish came, not from the disciples but from a young person. We could use this bit of information to remind ourselves as youth workers that our aim should be to let the young step forward. Even in small or cell groups ministries, it is possible to overlook young people's potential. When I had finally acknowledged that my own predictable programme of games interspersed with meaningful thoughts, was not scratching where my youth group were itching, I committed myself to equipping the young people in my care to minister to each other and to their world. After all, reaching other young people was their *mission*; mine was to help them achieve it.

Jesus called the disciples so 'that they might be with him and that he might send them out to preach' (Mk. 3:14). Approximately two years later, after his death, the persecuting authorities were forced to take note that these unschooled, ordinary men were indeed true followers of Jesus, faithfully continuing their teacher's life and work (Acts 4:13, 14). Jesus' strategy of focusing, not on the crowds, but on a small group of individuals, had worked. Now it was up to them to multiply his ministry.

Before moving on, take a moment to thank God for each young person in your care and for the gifts they have to offer. Then consider the wider needs of your community. How many spiritually hungry young people are there in your area? Jesus says to you, 'You give them something to eat.'

Moses

Fathers-in-law can be a great source of wisdom, and Moses was fortunate to have Jethro (Ex. 18:13–26). He could see that, unless he made some changes, Moses would eventually 'burn out' through sheer exhaustion. He was simply not physically or emotionally capable of ministering to all the varied needs of the Israelite people. If their spiritual growth was to be sustained, something had to change.

Jethro's solution was simple. He advised Moses to develop what in effect was a small or cell group ministry: leaders of groups of ten people were supported by leaders of fifties, who in turn were supported by leaders of hundreds, who were themselves supported by leaders of thousands. Through these small or cell groups, Moses was able to continue to be effective in his overall leadership and avoid the danger of collapsing due to overwork. As well as making life easier for Moses, the small or cell groups also had the advantage of developing leadership skills among those selected from 'all the people' to head them.

Peter

As youth workers, we often long for a sudden influx of new young people, then struggle to keep pace when there is one. Imagine Peter's reaction when, following his first public talk, *three thousand* people responded (Acts 2:41)! But Jesus had prepared him and his fellow disciples for this. They remembered the example he had given them, and immediately set about establishing a network of similar small or cell groups. Luke records that 'Every day they continued to meet together in the temple courts. They broke bread in their homes and ate together with glad and sincere hearts, praising God and enjoying the favour of all the people' (Acts 2:46, 47a). They were discovering that the bigger they grew, the smaller they had to feel.

Youth groups which experience sudden growth often need time to assimilate new people. This can result in temporary stagnation if they rely on one or two key leaders doing all the work, while the rest of the group is left to spectate. In Peter's experience, 'the Lord added to their number daily those who were being saved' (Acts 2:47b), and this growth continued (Acts 5:14). Without adopting a small or cell group ministry that encouraged every-member participation, it is hard to see how such growth could have been sustained.

Paul

Paul's conversion may have begun on the Damascus road, but the scales fell from his eyes three days later, in a house in the company of a few others (Acts 9:17–19). Presumably, God could have transformed him on the spot, but chose instead to involve a small band of ordinary people to play a part in the process. For the next two years, the support of this group became crucial to Paul. His fearsome reputation was such that not even the church in Jerusalem would believe at first that he had genuinely changed: it took the testimony of Barnabas, a fellow small-group member, to convince them.

Paul soon followed Jesus' example in gathering a small number of people about him. After spending time together, they would be dispatched to distant regions or, in some cases, left behind to establish new groups. In Lystra, the travelling small group was joined by Timothy, a young person from a mixed-race family (Acts 16:1–3) who, by the time they reached Berea, was ready to handle some responsibility (Acts 17:13–15) and was subsequently sent to settle problems at Corinth (1 Cor. 4:17). Later, Paul joined in a small group with seven others – Sopater, Aristarchus, Secundus, Gaius, Timothy, Tychicus and Trophimus (Acts 20:4, 5). It seems that wherever Paul went, so did his small group which, in turn, was used to establish new groups.

The presence of small or cell groups in the church is inferred in Paul's letters (1 Cor. 14:23): it seems that there were times when members of the church met separately, presumably in people's homes. The use of homes as meeting-places ensured that those groups remained small. Just how small would depend on the wealth of the house-owners. A moderately wealthy person's entertaining room would have held approximately thirty people, but the majority of new believers, who were not from wealthy backgrounds, would have had more modest homes.[8] Paul would also have been familiar with the Jewish stipulation that just ten people were required to form a synagogue.

He may have been a keen exponent of small or cell groups but, it appears, Paul was not the best small group communicator, particularly when young people were present. In Troas, one meeting became a Teach-a-thon 'as Paul talked on and on' for many hours (Acts 20:7–12). This was too much for one young man, Eutychus, who just couldn't stay awake. Unfortunately, he was perched near a window at the time, and fell three floors to his death. Paul stopped his talk to revive Eutychus; however, that done, he promptly returned to the small group and continued teaching until daylight. Now, selfishly seeking to avoid litigation, let me say that Paul's example should only be followed if you have confidence in the leader's ability to raise people from the dead!

Finally ...

What Moses foreshadowed, Jesus modelled and the early church multiplied. The book of Acts documents the phenomenal growth of the church as new believers met together, usually in small or cell groups in people's homes, and 'the Lord added to their number daily those who were being saved'. While it would be wrong to imply that small or cell groups were the only contributing factor to this growth, they certainly played a significant part. I believe that this provides us with a biblical mandate to develop small or cell groups ministries in the church today, and especially with young people.

Having established positive reasons for setting up a small-group ministry, we can now turn our attention to what is meant by small or cell groups – because they can mean different things to different people.

Homework

- Find out, from your local youth service, education or social services departments, how many young people live in your area.

....

....

- How many of these young people do you estimate have no connection with a church?

....

....

- Note down the names of five young people who you consider would benefit from being in your small group.

....

....

....

....

....

3

Small groups, big menu

Imagine for a moment you are hungry. You read a glowing review of a new restaurant in town. Eventually curiosity and hunger get the better of you, and you go in search of culinary excellence. A waiter seats you at a table and asks for your order. You say, 'I'd like some food, please.'

'Yes, certainly,' replies the waiter as he hands you the menu, 'but *what* would you like?' By now you may have built up an appetite for small or cell groups and be keen to get going. But what type of group would you want to choose? Some groups are temporary, others semi-permanent; some are activity-based, while others focus on a specific need. To help you decide, here is a menu detailing much of what is on offer.

Chez Small Groups

Starters

Breakaway groups
Interest groups
Service groups

Side orders

Pastoral groups
Support groups

Main courses

Ministry groups
Cell groups

Desserts

Self-select groups

Starters

For those wanting a quick snack, it is possible simply to order something from the starter menu. But customers should be aware that while these dishes often whet the appetite, they rarely satisfy long-term hunger.

Breakaway groups

Formed almost by chance, these groups have the short-est shelf-life. Typically, the youth worker, having served up a game and a meaningful thought, then asks the assembled young people to form themselves into small groups to complete a defined activity. This might include discussing a question, solving a problem or cre-ating a display. When the task is finished, the groups are disbanded. Subsequent activities usually result in differ-ent small group configurations being formed.

While these temporary small groups encourage the young people to mix together, they do not grow community, provide pastoral care or develop gifting. Those who select this starter often do so because they recognise the value of group work but fail to recognise that a well-organised small or cell group ministry has benefits beyond the length of an activity. Youth groups that have been ordering this starter should seriously consider trying a main course.

Interest groups

The overwhelming success of the Alpha Course in many UK churches has resulted in the production of two youth versions which aim, over a ten-week period, to introduce young people to Christianity. Usually, a small number meet together for a fixed period of time to consider the authenticity of the Christian faith. The group is then disbanded and the members integrated into the wider youth group. These 'taster' small or cell groups are often established because there is a sudden intake of new people into the wider group.

Many baptism or confirmation classes are, in reality, interest groups: they draw together a small number of people with a shared interest for a limited period of time. Many people remember with fondness not so much the programme they studied as the camaraderie they experienced during group meetings. These classes have the potential to become small or cell groups.

The success of an interest group will depend not just on the quality of the material used, but on the conducive nature of the group environment. If it allows difficult questions to be asked, each member can participate fully and significant attention can be given to individuals. However, the dilemma may be what to do once the course has finished. Not everyone will find it easy to integrate into the wider youth group. A simple solution may be to allow the temporary group to evolve into a fully-functioning small or cell group, thus continuing the good progress already made. Why stop something that is clearly working?

Service groups

There is something very powerful about a group of young people working together to serve the needs of others, particularly if this is done in the name of Christ. Tasks might include washing cars, visiting the house-bound, assisting with children's play-schemes or even serving with an overseas development agency. Oasis Youth Action enables groups of young people to gain 'hands-on' experience of community action for short periods of time in some of the UK's toughest inner cities.[9] As well as serving the needs of and learning from the local community, the small group environment enables the participants to experience a strong sense of belonging and a common purpose. While social action programmes provide a temporary small group experience, some service-based small or cell groups can be semi-permanent, with members participating over an extended period of time.

Side orders

Pastoral groups

This type of group comes as a surprise to young people because they rarely know of its existence. Recognising the need for greater pastoral care and delegation of responsibilities, the co-ordinating youth leader asks each member of the youth work team to take pastoral responsibility for a small number of young people. Members of the pastoral group are often unaware of the group's existence; to them it just seems coincidental that it always seems to be the same youth worker that takes such a positive interest in them.

In this case, it is the co-ordinating youth worker who benefits most. They are relieved from the pressure of having sole responsibility but enjoy the positive results that arise from the pastoral care. But the pastoral groups do not help the young people to develop because they never meet together as a group. Nor can they develop strong relationships with the youth leader. While this option is an improvement on the instant group, it is still tantalisingly short of a fully developed small or cell group. Sampling the pastoral group should inspire youth leaders to be more adventurous with their menu.

Support groups

Following a school presentation on bullying, a small group of young people asked to meet together on a regular basis to discuss related issues. None of the group members were Christians; what united them was their common experience of bullying. For some young people faced with a crisis such as drug addiction, bereavement or self-harm, support groups can be invaluable. Sometimes it is enough for Christians simply to stand with young people in their struggle rather than serve up quick-fix solutions.

All the above side orders have some benefits, but none provides enough to become the basis of an intentional small-group ministry. They are all either too temporary or too narrow to create something of lasting significance. Let's move on to consider three more options on our menu.

Main courses

Ministry groups

John Wimber, the American founder of the charismatic Vineyard movement, placed great emphasis on the supernatural and on the importance of community. The Vineyard 'kinship' groups stressed the need for peer ministry through the exercise of spiritual gifts. They found these groups were an ideal environment in which to develop or empower people. Reading from the Bible, praying out loud or leading worship all became less intimidating when done among a small number of close and supportive friends. Churches that carry the charismatic label often tend to favour this type of small group.

The advantage of this rather spicy dish is the semi-permanence of the groups. Pastoral care, participation and community are all encouraged. The young people know which group they belong to, who else is in it and who is responsible for developing it. The weakness, however, can be a tendency to become inward-focused, with new people, especially non-Christians, being discouraged from attending what appears to be an intense and at times 'wacky' group. As a result, numerical growth may be slow or even non-existent.

Cell groups

Small groups of various kinds have been around for centuries and have gone through a number of name changes, from John Wesley's 'class meetings' to the kinship groups described above. To these must now be added cell groups which, in turn, have given rise to the cell-church movement.

The basic aim of a cell group is to be an expression of church in the community, directed not by an all-powerful leader but by its own members. The broad purpose of cell churches is to welcome new people, enable them to apply the Bible to their lives, lead them in worship and, in turn, to enable them to grow by assimilating non-Christians ... and so on. This is certainly not a bad, if somewhat all-encompassing, aim! Central to the cell-church approach is the understanding that the life of the church is found, not in the big group or congregation but in the cell groups. The cells are the foundation upon which everything is built. For Paul Yonggi Cho and the Full Gospel Central Church in Seoul, South Korea, this is particularly crucial given that their country lives constantly under the threat of invasion from communist North Korea. Should this ever happen, they believe, their church buildings and key leaders may be destroyed but the church would live on in the cell groups.

In the cell-group model, the youth ministry is the sum total of all the cell groups; it is not just what happens at the Friday evening 'big group'. In effect, the 'big group' is simply the occasion when all the cell groups happen to be present at the same time. To put it simply, the cell groups are essential, but the youth club *per se* is not. This is a significant development in the understanding of small groups, which have in the past often been regarded as a beneficial but secondary element. Here the 'big group' supports the cell groups, not vice versa.

Cell churches are generally built on the following five values:

- Jesus is at the centre of the gathered believers and the individual Christian's life.

- Christian community is fostered through relationship.

- Each cell member can grow in their Christian walk and knowledge of God.

- Every cell member can be released to minister to others in the body of Christ.

- Every cell member can seek to bring others to Christ.

There is, I believe, much to commend cell groups to the connoisseur, and what follows in subsequent chapters supports the principles of this model. In contrast to the potentially inward-looking ministry groups, cell groups ensure that the group of young people remain outward-focused, with members constantly aiming to introduce new people. The emphasis on empowerment encourages a loyal commitment to the group and significant personal growth. (To find out more about cell groups, visit <www.cellchurch.co.uk>)

However, in applying the cell-church model to youth ministries, I believe it is still necessary to provide a 'big group' experience and, to be fair, this is widely accepted by most cell-church advocates. Many who follow the cell-group model provide weekly cells but only monthly big-group sessions. While I believe that small or cell groups are essential to the development of any youth ministry, they cannot meet all the physical, intellectual, social, emotional and spiritual needs of young people. Successful youth ministries are those that provide quality small or cell group *and* 'big group' experiences. Most Christian young people feel isolated enough without being cut off further from like-minded peers because they happen to be in other small or cell groups. It would therefore rarely be appropriate to develop a small or cell group ministry that didn't create regular opportunities for a cross-section of young people to meet as a whole group. For a balanced diet, this chef recommends giving equal prominence to both. Saying this does not detract from the significant role played by small or cell groups.

Proponents of the cell-group model generally follow the adult format and prescribe a very structured programme to ensure that each ninety-minute session includes the four basic elements of welcome, worship, word and witness. An initial welcoming 'icebreaker' helps members get to know each other and relax into the setting (thirty minutes); this is followed by 'worship' during which members focus on getting to know God better (twenty minutes). The 'word' is an application-centred ministry time rather than a Bible study, and usually tackles a single issue or question (twenty minutes); as for 'witness', the group members plan ways of helping each other share the faith with their friends.

If not applied sensitively, this approach can tend to favour Christian young people who are already conversant with worship and Bible study. I encourage those pursuing the cell-group model to consider also the wider needs of the unchurched; those on the fringe who are not yet sure they are ready for such an intense programme. Most radical movements are in danger of becoming institutional monoliths when there are formulas to follow and products to sell. I would hate to see this happen to the cell-group movement.

Desserts

Having studied this menu, you may decide that what you most want is a big and varied portion from the dessert section. Before guilt takes hold, let me say this is not as naughty as it may seem.

Self-select groups

These provide opportunities for interested young people to opt in to – or out of – small or cell groups of their choice. One option is to offer young people the opportunity to join a small or cell group, whilst still maintaining the 'big group' for everyone else. In a youth group of twenty, perhaps twelve may participate in a total of two small or cell groups, with the remainder taking part in other activities.

On the positive side, this twin-track approach ensures that young people are given choice. It also enables the youth workers to deduce the level and nature of young people's interest. It enables committed young people to develop in an encouraging and hassle-free environment. Negatively, however, it can be divisive and elitist, with those who are not participating feeling left out. This approach does not foster community either, as those who need it most are often those that opt out. As we have seen, the cell-group model, with its high level of commitment and Christian content, does not always help young people on the fringe. For them something else is required.

A more constructive way forward may be for the youth ministry to comprise a feast of small or cell groups. This enables young people to select the type of group that best suits their needs. I personally like this arrangement as it promotes choice and diversity. Those wanting a discipleship environment could opt for cell groups, while interest groups may be more appropriate for those seeking faith, leaving those who require a more robust and practical expression of faith to opt for service groups. For young people on the fringe, simply participating in a small group that provides social activities could be a significant step. In the next chapter I will advocate having 'no rules'.

Finally...

These, then, are the dishes on offer at *Chez Small Groups*. Which will you choose? There are those who will always order the same dish no matter what else is on the menu, simply because they know it will satisfy them. They don't see the need to try anything new because they are happy with what they already have. But they run the risk of missing out on something better, more exciting, different. You won't know how good a dish is until you try it. Perhaps now is the time to try something new and exotic.

To help you reflect on your final choice, here are some questions for you to look at. Then we will move on to consider who should be in a small group, and ask how small is 'small?'

Homework

• What dish, if any, do you currently order from Chez Small Groups? How effectively does it meet the needs of all your young people?

....

....

• Where in your youth ministry is there the potential to develop a small or cell group ministry?

....

....

- From the menu, what dish would you consider to be the most appropriate for your youth ministry, and why?

....

....

- List the names of five young people you are most concerned to reach through a small or cell groups ministry.

....

....

....

....

....

4

Small groups, big membership

Monday mornings were bad enough, but Monday mornings in the winter were awful. Standing on a frozen rugby pitch in an oversized rugby shirt was not my idea of fun – but apparently it was character-building. Those who genuinely liked the game, and who were good enough to be picked for the school teams, would spend their time running up and down the far pitch, making very butch noises. The loudest noises I produced came from my chattering teeth or were exclamations of panic whenever the wretched ball found me. I hated rugby and would do everything possible to avoid playing. Everyone else always seemed so much more athletic or robust than me.

Dividing into teams was always a traumatic experience. I can still remember standing awkwardly on the touchline, waiting to be 'selected', knowing that the team which picked me would already consider itself to have lost. I didn't want to play, but neither did I want to be excluded. (Needless to say, I didn't go on to play for the British Lions.)

Some young people feel just as awkward when they first come to the youth group. Everyone else seems so confident and capable, and when the leader asks the group to get into teams they fear that they'll be left standing on the 'touchline'. Establishing the right chemistry in a small group is essential to its future success, so in this chapter we will answer some of the questions surrounding membership. Which young people should get picked for what group? How many are required for each group? Does it matter what gender they are? Should novices be placed with veterans?

Before answering these questions, I want to make it clear that I do not believe small or cell groups are necessarily the same as house groups. These seem to be geographically based Bible study groups, a dozen or more people united together by postcode – and usually not a lot else! Some people have had a very positive experience of these groups; others have not. For me, being told what to study, when and with whom is too inflexible. You and your fellow youth workers may need to put aside once and for all any thoughts of introducing more youth-friendly versions of house groups.

No rules

If you feel that the various rules – of time, day, membership and material – restrict small or cell group membership, why not simply say there are no rules? Young people can join any group of their choice; small or cell groups can do whatever works for them; they can meet when and as often as they like. The small or cell groups can consist of friends, people of a similar age or background, members of a band or drama team, or just about any other combination the young people choose.

Cliques are often considered to be 'the enemy', but the 'no rules' principle assumes that cliques can, in fact, be positive. If five young friends want to join the youth group, the last thing I'll do is split them up into different groups – unless, of course, that's what they want! To separate them would be to risk losing them all. Instead, by having them form their own small or cell group, not only do they remain involved but there is also every chance that other friends may want to get involved as well.

I came into contact with Jonathan whilst I was youth worker at Altrincham Baptist Church, in Greater Manchester. He became involved with the youth ministry as a result of a visit to his school by the Worldwide Message Tribe. After going to three concerts, he decided he wanted 'in', whatever that was, and joined the 14+ youth programme. Within a few weeks many of his school friends had joined him. Almost immediately a new small group, comprising this peer group, was formed.

I have generally adopted a 'no rules' approach to group work; young people can be in any small or cell group of their choice. This is not as anarchic as might at first sound. The 'no rules' principle enables young people to retain control of their own groups: nothing is forced upon them; nor are they required to do anything they feel uncomfortable with. It treats young people with respect and gives them a voice. The 'no rules' principle is particularly important during the development of a small or cell groups ministry. It reassures those who fear that small or cell groups will be used to separate them from their friends in some 'divide and rule' conspiracy that they will be able to be in a group of their choosing. It is therefore important to allow the few who want to change groups to do so without feeling they are failures or somehow less worthy.

Run-a-round

The 'no rules' principle should add value to a small or cell group ministry, not detract from it. However, constant membership changes can undermine its relational purpose. A group that, each week, comprises different people will never grow community. There is, however, a simple solution. If you are old enough to remember Mike Reid's Run-a-Round TV show, I have some bad news for you – you're no longer young! If the title means nothing to you, let me explain how the game worked. For every question asked, there would be three possible solutions, each represented by a letter. The young contestants would have to stand under the letter they believed represented the correct answer. However, there would then be a further three seconds to 'run-a-round' when, if they wanted to, they could change their answers.

I have found it helpful to declare the first two weeks of each term as 'run-a-round', during which young people have an opportunity to change groups. At the end of this period members must remain with their group until the next 'run-a-round' opportunity. This ensures that the 'no rules' principle does not undermine the stability and consistency of the groups whilst still allowing opportunity for young people to effect change.

The small print

For control freaks like me, the prospect of 'no rules' can at first appear quite intimidating, even a short cut to disaster. Surely it will lead to chaos and lack of direction, and does 'no rules' really mean 'no involvement'? To counter these concerns, two things must be remembered.

First, freedom is usually found within boundaries, not outside them. Once, as an experiment, psychologists monitored children playing in the playground of an American inner-city school. They observed how the children made full use of all the open space, right up to the wire fence. The psychologists decided to remove the fence. They discovered that this time the children seemed to huddle together and play in a much smaller area, as far away as they could get from where the fence had been. The psychologists concluded that the boundary provided the children with much greater freedom. In promoting 'no rules', you usually need a few general guidelines, or boundaries, to enhance the groups rather than hinder them. For myself, I generally look for small or cell groups to be small (naturally!) and single sex (for reasons I'll explain later).

Second, implementing 'no rules' requires an energetic, servant-style of leadership in which the ministry leader seeks to influence and support the small or cell groups rather than dictate to them. This requires an investment of time and the belief that those directly involved in the groups are best placed to know what is right for them. Overseeing a small-group ministry is not like winding up a clock which then ticks away without assistance. Every small group I have been involved with has had an in-built inertia which, if the group was left to its own devices, would cause it to cease operating. Small or cell groups need constant attention, but this is best given through serving them rather than by dictating to them.

Group membership

John Buckeridge, writing in *Youthwork Magazine*,[10] quoted a senior staff member of a market research company as saying that their 'young people's focus groups always consist of a minimum six, maximum eight members of the same sex and of an identical age.' The reason for this was because 'if we have more than eight or mix the sexes or ages they stop being honest. They spend most of the time posing or pretending. We want them to say what they really think and be really open with us.' There is a lot of wisdom in this, as I will now explain.

Size matters

Just as there is a range of dishes in *Chez Small Groups*, so there is a variety of portions to suit most appetites. At the risk of sounding basic, the primary qualification of a small group must be that it is small – yet frequently I come across groups that are nothing of the sort. Many churches which once fought hard to introduce house groups have stopped fighting to maintain them and, as a result, have groups with high membership levels and low attendance. The development of an oversized small or cell group is not a sign of success but failure, and should be avoided at all costs. What, then, is the ideal size?

I personally believe small-group membership should be kept within single figures, with five being the optimum number. Less than four, and the group ceases to be a group; more than nine, and it ceases to be small. This is not a rule, but I have found it a helpful way of ensuring that small group dynamics are maintained.

It is, of course, possible to be overlooked in an overgrown small group. Next time you are in a group setting, observe the contribution each participant makes. Note who is dominating the group and who is dominated by it. Try conducting an experiment to determine at what size a group begins to feel impersonal. Having two

people begin a debate of their choice and gradually
introducing new participants one at a time can do this.
Bring along some observers whose job it is to record the
dynamics, paying particular attention to individual contributions and body language. Ask both the participants
and the observers to determine at what size they
thought the group ceased to be personal and inclusive.
Bigger groups generally provide more opportunities for
people either to be excluded or to excuse themselves
from fully participating and, as such, do not grow community.

One criticism of having small or cell groups *too* small
is that absenteeism may render them not viable. This can
be a problem, but not as much as you might think. A
group of twelve will generally have a higher percentage
of non-attendees than a group half that size. This is
because those in the smaller group know their attendance is crucial, while members of larger groups may
assume their non-attendance will go unnoticed. Total
attendance tends to be greater in four groups of five than
in two groups of ten (or one group of twenty). It is also
worth bearing in mind that groups with double figure
memberships can experience logistical difficulties relating to transportation and securing an appropriate meet-
ing-place.

Gender matters

It is at this point that I embrace seemingly Victorian values and recommend single-sex groups. When I first
introduced this at Altrincham Baptist Church it is fair to
say young people expressed some initial reservations.
However, within six months they became ardent sup-
porters of the principle. So much so that, when some
years later, a group of young people wanted to form a

mixed-sex group, it was the other young people – not the youth workers – that objected. The 'no rules' principle compelled us to enable the formation of a mixed group. But, within a couple of months, the group folded.

Single-sex groups enable young people to talk with confidence about personal issues, including relationships, in a way that would be impossible if in the presence of the opposite sex. Young lads in particular seem to profit from not having to act out a stereotypical role for the benefit of girls. Furthermore, a small group that includes two (or more) dating members can unsettle the group dynamics, particularly if the relationship ends. Though both sexes deserve equal respect and opportunities, it would be wrong to assume they have the same needs. The majority of males still seem to prefer a more physical and robust approach in the group, whereas females are generally more comfortable in feelings-based activities.

Single-sex small or cell groups can become difficult to maintain if the 'big group' is not given sufficient prominence. Without a regular opportunity to interact in a larger setting with members of the opposite sex can hinder young people's ability to form friendships, as well as more exclusive relationships, with members of the opposite sex. It is for this reason that those who opt for a purer version of the cell-group model often have to adopt mixed-sex groups. This places additional strain on recruitment levels, as each mixed-sex small group requires, not one but two leaders – one male, the other female. This is non-negotiable. This may require the merger of two groups into one, resulting in a larger group size and a corresponding loss of intimacy. In short, mixed-sex groups can be achieved, but at what cost?

Having said this, the cyber small group referred to in Chapter 1 was a mixed-sex group. Set up by young people who were leaving home for the first time to go to university, this group generated its own sense of community via the Internet. I claim it was their mature age which enabled them to be a mixed-sex group; they say it was because of the huge distances that separated them! I mention this to acknowledge the different needs of those in their twenties, should your definition of 'young' stretch that far. So much, then, for age and gender – what of the committed and non-committed?

Core members

All small or cell groups need to have a core membership of young people who are committed to achieving the aims of their group. The most committed are often the ones whose own journey has been significantly aided by small or cell groups. Essentially, they are the ones who can be relied on to attend meetings and to make the most of whatever is on offer. They actively seek to recruit new people to the group, then often go on to lead dynamic small or cell groups of their own.

Whether or not core members are believers will largely depend on the type of small group they are in. An interest group used in an Alpha Course may initially contain few believers but still have a significant number of core members whose attendance is regular and who participate fully. The issue is not what people believe but how committed they are to the aims of the group.

Fringe members

Lighting a room to create a range of moods can be a challenge if you have a traditional on/off switch that allows for only two states. But add a dimmer switch and suddenly its 'Hello, Dolly!' The room can be in total darkness, dazzling light and all shades in between – the choice is yours. Some small or cell groups struggle to create the right mood because they only allow for two states: 'in' (Christian) or 'out' (not). This type of pigeonholing may exclude a range of people – friends and relatives of core members, the offspring of churchgoing parents who have not as yet connected with the youth ministry. Such young people are neither anti-faith nor pro-faith: they are undecided, on the fringe.

Frequency

You may want to extend the 'no rules' principle to include the frequency of group gatherings. However, there is a need for at least some boundaries. A small or cell group that meets too infrequently will never reach its potential, and I suggest that anything less than fortnightly falls into this category. How much more frequently the group should meet will depend on the availability of both the leaders and the members. A pattern I have found helpful is to ensure small or cell groups meet weekly during term time – one week on their own and the other week during a 'big group' session formed by all the small or cell groups joining together. For this second week, the groups could meet as part of a youth congregation or service. This pattern limits the commitment required of group leaders and ensures that once a fortnight each group is visible to the ministry co-ordinator. This, in turn, aids evaluation and supervision. The key is to develop a rhythm that best suits your own situation.

In the next chapter, we will be considering some of the issues relating to small or cell-group leaders.

Homework

- If you decided to adopt a 'no rules' policy, what 'small print' would you consider it necessary to add?

....

....

....

....

....

- List the names of young people in your youth ministry who you consider to be core members in your preferred type(s) of small group.

....

....

....

....

....

- List the names of young people in your youth ministry who you consider to be fringe members in your preferred type(s) of small group.

....

5

Small groups, big leaders

Three years after leaving Bible College I faced a major challenge. Rob was not well enough to be Father Christmas for the play-group children, and I was the only other male available. I could think of many reasons why I shouldn't be Santa, and none of them were theological. I am tall and thin, and the outfit was clearly for someone small and round. I am also the most wooden of actors and couldn't pull off a convincing 'Ho, ho, ho!' if my life depended on it. Worst of all, I didn't have any boots – I was about to become the first Father Christmas in Reeboks! This was not going to be an easy gig.

All the children were seated in the room, eagerly awaiting the magical arrival of Father Christmas. There wasn't a dry eye – or bottom – in the room as I stumbled in, carrying my bin-liner containing all the presents. 'Ho, ho ... er ... er (cough) ho, ho, ho!' I blurted out. I was performing to the most intimidating of audiences – fifty two- to four-year-olds – and I was petrified! Over an hour later I emerged from the room a physical and emotional wreck. I had just become responsible for delivering numerous train sets, puppies, bicycles and My Little

Ponies, not to mention a couple of new brothers and a dad – all in the course of one night, and in person.

As I am not used to working with such young children, it was not surprising that I found them intimidating. Many find young people equally so. But small or cell groups ministries rely on finding the right leaders, so how do we go about recruiting (and keeping) such people? Many small or cell groups ministries find it helpful to involve young people as peer leaders. I will cover this in Chapter 7. For now, small-group leaders are assumed to be adult.

Requirements

Some youth groups, in desperation, accept into youth ministry the first person with a pulse. However, this communicates poor regard either for the young people or for the volunteer. Bear in mind that it can be very difficult to remove a leader once they are *in situ*! Much better to take time at the start to consider exactly what kind of leader(s) you require.

The *Play Station* ride at Blackpool Pleasure Beach provides a few seconds of utter terror (often followed by weeks of bragging). However, before the ride can blast off, three attendants must each give the 'thumbs-up' or the ride goes nowhere. Before a small-group leader can be launched into ministry, let me suggest they must display three requirements before getting the 'thumbs-up'.

Faith

Being in Christian ministry, I would want to know that all the small-group leaders I work with are dedicated followers of Christ. By this I mean that they have a genuine desire to see God at work in their lives and are willing to trust him as they work through their struggles. It is important that leaders are prepared to be honest about their own spirituality with the young people: this creates a healthy, open environment in which real issues can be tackled and faith can grow.

Belonging

I would also want to know that the leaders have a high regard for the church and are active participants in the local congregation. A leader who speaks negatively of the church, or whose attendance at worship services is erratic, will not inspire the young people they are responsible for. It is important that each leader has the support of the church leadership and, ultimately, is accountable to it.

Passion

In addition, leaders should have a healthy passion for young people. They do not necessarily need to be the greatest of youth communicators or experts in 'youth culture', but they must be genuinely interested. Nothing impresses young people more than adults who demonstrate a real concern for them. A small-group leader who invests time with individual young people will soon gain much respect. While most skills can be developed, all potential leaders must be inherently 'good with people'.

The three 'thumbs up' characteristics outlined above can be a useful measure of someone's suitability for small-group leadership, but they don't guarantee it. The person may not actually have a calling to such a ministry. This can only be discerned through discussion and prayer.

Finally, there is one last test which must be passed before someone can be entrusted with a small group of young people.

Good practice

In our mad, crazy world, it is no longer acceptable to take risks with the safety of young people by appointing workers without first ensuring they can be trusted. The onus is on would-be volunteers to prove their suitability. Small or cell groups are potentially susceptible to abuse – activities often take place outside regular session times. Young people and parents must be reassured that every precaution has been taken. This is 'good practice'.

The government's current advice for voluntary groups is based on the publication *Safe From Harm*[11] which, in turn, has been incorporated into various denominational papers.[12] These recommend the following:

The organisation should adopt a policy statement on safeguarding the welfare of young people.

The work of the organisation should be planned so as to minimise the situations where abuse may occur.

There should be a system in place whereby young people can talk with an independent person whenever they wish.

Agreed procedures for the protection of young people should apply to all paid staff and volunteers.

Clear rules should be given to all paid staff and volunteers.

The organisation should use supervision as a means of protecting young people.

The organisation should treat all would-be paid staff and volunteers as job applicants for any position that involves contact with young people.

Each applicant should have at least one reference from someone who has experience of the applicant's paid work or volunteering with young people.

The organisation should explore all applicants' experience of working or contact with young people in an interview before making an appointment.

The organisation should find out whether an applicant has any conviction for criminal offences against young people.

Paid voluntary appointments should be made conditional upon the successful completion of a probationary period.

Guidelines should be issued as to how to deal with the disclosure or discovery of abuse.

Paid staff and volunteers, their line-managers and policymakers should be trained in the prevention of abuse.

Though following these recommendations may appear bureaucratic, I have never had an adverse reaction from a potential small-group leader and only encouragement from parents. Increased administration is a small price to pay for peace of mind.

Useful extras

Though not prerequisite, there are a number of skills that can be a real bonus and are therefore worth looking out for in potential small-group leaders.

Organisation

An effective leader will, among other things, want to organise regular times and places for the group to meet, to celebrate events like birthdays and be in regular contact with young people on the fringe. All this requires a level of personal discipline not always attributed to youth workers!

Special interest

One of the ways busy workers can foster a rapport with their young people is by involving them in their hobbies and interests. A newly-appointed small-group leader once told me of his plans to invite his group to go scuba-diving with him. An afternoon spent walking in the hills can often achieve more than a whole day in a more formal setting, with both the young people and group leader gaining a better appreciation of each other. Making use of interests and hobbies enables leaders to play to their strengths and often results in young people trying activities they might never have considered before.

Communication skills

Many people coming into church-based youth work tend to be distracted by the need to deliver a message or Sunday School-style lesson. Though most small or cell groups are not essentially teaching groups, it will still be helpful for group leaders to have creative communication skills. With such a small audience, there is no room for lectures or seminar notes. Some of the most effective communicators inspire their young group members with their use of illustrations. Good examples of this can be seen in the Hollywood film, *Dead Poets Society*, in which Robin Williams plays the part of a progressive schoolmaster who uses different locations and activities to inspire his pupils. The skill is not in delivering the main teaching points but in making them come alive in the hearts and minds of the group members. More of this later.

Recruitment

Many are called to youth work but few are chosen. And even fewer, it seems, volunteer – most groups I know are understaffed by over-stretched youth workers. The biggest challenge lies not in attracting the right young people but in attracting the right youth worker – it is not the harvest but the harvesters who are in short supply. Faced with this reality, developing a small-group ministry may seem like a luxury few youth groups can afford. But such a ministry actually provides increased recruitment potential.

Many people don't volunteer for youth ministry because they have a wrong impression of what is involved. They imagine a youth worker to be someone who, after a busy day at work, emerges from a telephone box as Superleader – faster than a flying snooker ball and stronger than an entire basketball team; able at a moment's notice to organise, teach and counsel young people! But Superleaders rarely make good small-group leaders. Most effective workers are those who simply invest their time and energy in a few individuals. By asking potential volunteers to care for just five young people, youth ministry becomes more manageable and accessible.

Effective recruitment is vital to any aspiring ministry; without a steady influx of new leaders, growth will soon be hindered. Traditional approaches to recruitment, which rely on one or two individuals finding and 'vetting' all candidates, can rarely keep pace with a growing ministry. One simple solution is to encourage all existing small-group leaders to share in the responsibility of recruitment. For anyone who has felt the strain of being responsible for staffing whole ministries, this is liberating. The rationale behind shared responsibility is the belief that every person has a sphere of influence, covering their friends and acquaintances, and it is from this pool that new leaders often emerge. The more recruiters, the larger the number of potential volunteers.

For this approach to work, small or cell group leaders need to be given simple guidelines to help them in their search for new volunteers. Providing a simple information sheet about volunteering in the youth ministry can empower existing small-group leaders to recruit others. Such sheets have the dual benefit of making the introduction easier for the small-group leader and ensuring that all potential recruits receive the same basic information.

One final reason why people are often reluctant to volunteer is the fear that once they commit themselves they will be trapped for life. I generally advocate recruiting people to serve for just one year at a time, in the belief that it will take volunteers six months to realise whether small or cell group leadership is for them or not. If it isn't, they will only have six months to go. This has to be better than getting a letter from someone informing you of their resignation with immediate effect, which leaves you struggling to find an instant replacement. It is comforting for each leader to know that each year, probably in May, they will be asked if they would like to continue in the new ministry year. They will also know that they are not being taken for granted. This approach does, of course, run the risk of promoting short-term service, but invariably it results in leaders serving longer than they might otherwise have done. With the bulk of recruitment taking place in the summer term, it allows for some creative approaches and high-profile campaigns.

Function

The prospect of leading a small or cell group can initially seem daunting, with the first few weeks being particularly difficult, especially if support is not forthcoming. Many new leaders worry about whether or not the young people will accept them, or how far they should seek to be involved in their lives. It will help if leaders have a clear understanding of what their responsibilities are and what they can expect in return.

Job descriptions are standard practice for paid employees but can be of equal benefit for volunteers. They explain clearly what is expected, why the task is so important and how volunteers can be sure they are doing the task well. For those who struggle with management theory in the church, it is sensible to soften the language and refer instead to 'ministry recognitions' or 'ministry descriptions'.

What you put in the job description will depend on what you and the other leaders believe to be achievable. Judy, who led one of my first small or cell groups, did so well that she inadvertently discouraged others from volunteering. Prospective group leaders saw the amount of time and energy she invested and concluded that if that was what being a small-group leader involved, perhaps they would join the choir after all. Better, therefore, to be realistic.

Essentially, small or cell group leaders have the primary task of serving and caring for the young people in their groups and must assume that if they don't, no one else will. Not for them the reward for good conduct or sign of special favour, but a commitment to serve their group's needs sacrificially. As will be seen later, an individual may be the leader but the group remains 'in charge', for it is the members who should determine the direction and style of the group.

Youth Ministry Description

This church takes very seriously your God-given calling to work with young people/children, and recognises the following to be your ministry:

Name: ....

Function: Small/Cell Group Leader

Programme: 15–19s

Purpose: To develop a small/cell group into a growing community of young people dedicated to loving Christ and serving his world.

Duration: 1 year, commencing 1 September.

Responsible to: Oasis Small/Cell Groups Co-ordinator

Duties:

- Be a dedicated follower of Christ.
- Aim to have weekly contact with core small/cell group members. This might be as a result of their attendance at the 15–19s programme, participation in a small group activity, conversation at a church event, a telephone call, a letter or a one-to-one meeting.
- Attend 15–19s sessions and lead a fortnightly small/cell group activity as required (materials will be provided).
- Aim to provide a fortnightly small/cell group activity that takes place outside regular 15–19s sessions. This should reflect the needs of the group and develop fellowship, worship, mission and/or discipleship.
- Recruit and encourage an assistant leader, thus promoting growth and small/cell group multiplication.
- Attend the 15–19s team meeting (monthly), plenary youth workers' gathering (termly) and a residential development weekend (annually).
- Aim to have occasional contact with parent(s) of small/ cell group members (termly).
- Actively encourage small-group members to understand and participate in the 15–19s vision, mission and strategy.

However, defining what each small-group leader should actually do is not always easy. In my desire to see that every young person was given a basic level of pastoral care, I once drew up a very detailed job description that even specified which day in the week follow-up calls were to be made. Though it made perfect sense to me as I typed it out in my office, it confused many of the leaders, who simply weren't used to such a regimented and hierarchical approach. In the workplace, management theory of an earlier era left nothing to chance. Every minute detail of every person's task was controlled and written down. So long as every worker stuck to the system, everything would be fine. The problem, however, was that it did nothing to develop initiative or innovation, and assumed that 'bosses' always knew better than 'workers'. Now companies recognise the importance of empowering their workforces to think for themselves, and many youth workers will come expecting to use their initiative. A good job description should provide them with plenty of scope and minimal detail. After all, they will know what is the best strategy for their young people.

You might want to model your job description on the above example.

Definition of success:

- All small-group members feel valued, supported and included.

- Young people are given opportunities for service and increasing responsibility to develop their own activities.

- Numerical growth leading to the formation of new small/cell groups.

Assistant leaders

As well as a designated leader, each small or cell group should aim to have an assistant who is a potential leader in the making. Some volunteers are apprehensive about taking on responsibility, even for just a few young people, but being an assistant can seem more manageable. Quite often, once they have gained in confidence, they will feel more positive about taking on extra responsibility.

Young people are rarely impressed by titles or roles. What matters to them is whether or not they like the person. It is therefore unrealistic to expect a small group to welcome immediately someone new and unknown just because they carry the title of 'Small Group Leader'. Quite rightly, they will need time to decide if this person can be trusted, is good to hang around with and is genuinely interested in them. Few leaders can communicate all this in less than a couple of months. Bringing an assistant into the group provides ample opportunity for the leader-in-waiting to develop a rapport with the young people, so that when a new group is ready to be formed a suitable leader is already in place.

Assistants become more important as the small or cell group grows. Investing time and energy in four young people can be demanding; to do the same for nine can be exhausting. Having additional support will be very welcome. Assistants need to feel a valued and necessary part of the team: if they are under-used, the message they receive is that they are not needed.

Homework

- List five positive reasons why some of your friends and acquaintances might want to join you in taking an interest in a few young people.

....

....

....

- Record the names of five people you know who may be suitable, and willing, to take an interest in a few young people. Pledge to contact them within the next two weeks.

Name	Telephone	Contacted

- Draw up your own small-group leader's job description

My function is: ....

My group is: ....

I will serve for: ....

My duties are: ....

....

....

....

....

....

I am successful when: ....

....

....

....

6

Small groups, big responsibility

From a distance, the rock-face didn't seem too great a challenge. Standing underneath, it looked very different – steep, extremely high and dangerous to attempt. As the noise level increased among the rest of the party, I became aware of my own silence: fear and adrenaline were gradually taking control of my body. In a vain attempt to maintain respect, I adopted the 'been there, done that' approach and, with a servant heart, let the other novice climbers go first. Nevertheless, as hard as I tried, I simply couldn't see any alternative to going where others more agile than I had gone before.

With the rest of the group safely at the summit, the instructor gave the signal for me to start climbing. To my relief, the first section was easier than expected, and I soon gained confidence. Then, suddenly and quite inexplicably, I found myself stuck. I couldn't go up but, at the same time, I dared not go down either. With arms and legs spread out in an undignified and uncomfortable position, I clung to the rock-face, reflecting on my predicament. It was too good an opportunity for the others to waste, however, and they were soon taunting me and offering less-than-helpful advice. In the meantime, I was beginning to panic.

It came as an immense relief to feel a tug on my harness and to hear the reassuring words of the instructor telling me that he had firm hold of me on the safety rope. He didn't have to do or say much else; I was just happy to know he was there. Eventually I was able to clear my head and pull myself up.

All those involved in a small or cell groups ministry need to know they are supported and that, if they slip, someone will be there to catch them. This is true for members and leaders, novices and veterans. Leading a small group is challenging and, if done conscientiously, the demand on time, emotions and energy can be high. While great personal satisfaction can be gained from seeing a small group grow and multiply, this alone cannot sustain someone in ministry.

Structure

Providing adequate support and pastoral care has little to do with being nice. An intentional small or cell group ministry is different from a numerically small youth group in that it plans to grow and develops a structure to promote growth. It considers who will care for the small-group leaders, how this will be achieved and what will happen when the number of small or cell groups has significantly increased.

When I first introduced small or cell groups in my church I did not provide the leaders with sufficient support and interpreted no news as good news. Later, it emerged that only half the groups were functioning at anything like their potential, while the rest were barely existing. Some leaders hadn't understood what was required of them; others didn't know how to apply the theory to their small or cell groups. Simply providing them with some basic inspiration and a job description was not enough; they needed someone to ask them challenging questions. How were they doing in their own spiritual journey? What were they doing with their small group? What were they hoping to see happen in the coming months?

Appointing a small-groups co-ordinator is one way of providing leaders with this kind of support. This person should possess an organised mind, have experience of leading a successful small group and the confidence of the other leaders. By establishing a rapport with the leaders, the co-ordinator will know what kind of support they require and how best to deliver it. Just as the leaders serve their groups, so the co-ordinator should serve the leaders, not seek to control them. Small or cell groups do not all function in the same way or have the same goals, so the co-ordinator will need to encourage individual leaders to be responsive to the needs of their groups. It is a case of giving them sufficient rope on which to swing but not enough to hang themselves with.

An athlete will only wear what is necessary or beneficial for their performance – anything more would be a hindrance. A manufacturer will only purchase expensive machinery if it can be shown to enhance the final product – otherwise it would be inefficient. In both examples, the key is 'added value'. Similarly, a small group co-ordinator must add value to what is already being achieved by the small or cell groups. A conscientious small group co-ordinator will enable leaders to be more successful than they might have been had the co-ordinator not been involved.

If, initially, your youth ministry consists of just one small group, then support could be sought from a general church leader such as an elder or deacon. But, as the number of groups multiplies, someone with more time and energy will be required. However, even a co-ordinator is unlikely to be able to support a double-figure number of small-group leaders and so, as the ministry grows, additional appointments will have to be made. Consideration should then focus on who sup- ports the co-ordinators.

At the Willow Creek Community Church in Chicago, it is maintained that ideally no one should have to care for much more than five people, and this applies to all areas of ministry. At Student Impact, the senior high ministry, five young people are cared for by a small-group leader; five small-group leaders are cared for by a campus director; five campus directors are cared for by an employed division director; and the division direc- tors are all cared for by the ministry's executive director. This structure has evolved over more than twenty-five years, having begun with just one small group. Originators of the cell-group model propose a similar structure but prefer the more sci-fi language of Cell Servants, Zone Servants and Zone Pastors. Precise titles are irrelevant; it is the provision of a supportive struc- ture covering all ministry members that is so vital.

Support should not just focus on demands and responsibilities; it should also communicate apprecia- tion for what small-group leaders are doing. As young people are not always forthcoming in thanking those who serve them, and parents are often unaware of the time and energy invested, it is important that leaders receive encouragement from elsewhere. This is a signifi- cant part of a co-ordinator's role, but it should not be left to them alone. Leaders should be encouraged to affirm each other and church members invited to add their own contribution.

In my church practice I have scheduled opportunities to take all those involved in youth and children's ministry away for a weekend together. As well as training and team building, these retreats provide an opportunity to thank the workers for all that they do. Another idea I picked up from a fellow youth worker was the value of using postcards to send encouraging messages to individuals on an ongoing basis. I always carry a selection in my case, and write them as particular people come into my mind. They are a simple and quick way of showing that I am aware and appreciative of what people are doing. Others use e-mail in the same way.

Personal development

Very few people are born leaders. Most are developed through a process of training, experience and encouragement. It is a mistake to assume that people automatically know how to lead a small group – very often they don't. An intentional small or cell group ministry must therefore consider appropriate ways of developing its leadership skills, for it will only be as successful as its leaders.

Programme a computer to follow a particular formula, and it will perform complex calculations with apparent ease. But faced with a variation in just one part of that formula, the computer will be rendered utterly useless. Computers are not capable (as yet) of thinking for themselves and must rely on human operators to tell them what to do. Even those with 'artificial intelligence' are only following instructions contained in their original programme. Similarly, some training methods imply that trainees have little intelligence of their own and must be provided with formulas to enable them to perform the required tasks. Formula-based training does not prepare people to think for themselves; rather, it ensures that they carry out orders and respond to problems in predetermined ways. This approach fails as soon as trainees leave the predictability of the classroom and are confronted by a new set of circumstances or challenges.

Rather than punching in formulas, it is probably better to focus on principles and encourage leaders to use these, along with their acquired experience, to think for themselves. The trainer's role is to help trainees learn, and this can usually be done with minimal direct intervention. Most opportunities for developing the right skills arise not in classrooms but as a result of informal conversation or a request for support. Rather than sitting people in rows and lecturing them, it may be far more productive to follow Jesus' example and use everyday situations to create natural learning opportunities. Together, leaders could share their own successes and failures, and agree on some helpful tips. Often, a well-focused question can have greater educational impact than a statement loaded with data, as it forces trainees to discover the resources that exist within themselves.

Accountability

An absence of accountability is now considered to have precipitated the downfall of the much-maligned Nine O'Clock Service (NOS) and its founder, the Reverend Chris Brain.[13] What began as a radical and well-respected attempt to reach young people in Sheffield disillusioned by the institutional church, became corrupted by Brain's charismatic personality and his abuse of position. NOS's growing popularity was matched only by increasing signs of folly, but those in a position to question Brain failed to do so. No one, it seems, wanted to interfere with something that was obviously meeting the needs of young people. But all was not well. Soon every news bulletin in Britain was full of revelations about the abuse and control that had gone on. Chris Brain went into hiding, the NOS was disbanded, and many sincere people came out damaged as a result.

Just because I have not heard of abuse in a small or cell groups ministry does not mean to say it could never happen. I value small or cell groups, but also recognise their inherent vulnerability. Much of what a group does takes place outside 'big group' sessions, and the potential for abuse is always present. Intentional small-group ministries need to be proactive in reducing this risk.

If the NOS and Chris Brain had been made accountable, the former might have survived and the latter might still be in successful ministry today. As it is, those with a wider leadership responsibility failed to ask challenging questions and, in so doing, denied those involved adequate pastoral care. Small-group leaders have a right to expect those who support them to ask difficult and probing questions, and to feel neglected if this doesn't happen. Group members can choose to make themselves accountable to each other, though their leaders cannot and should not insist on this. However, leaders automatically choose to be accountable the moment they accept responsibility for their groups. I would not allow a small-group leader to continue in ministry if they refused to be held accountable for their conduct and character. Likewise, a co-ordinator should be free to visit any small group at any time and to ask any question of any member. This should prevent groups from becoming closed to outside inspection.

Emergency exit

The movie, *A Few Good Men*, highlighted the danger of
what can happen when authority is used to suppress
personal freedom and values. In this story, US Marine
Corps soldiers were required to abide by their all-
important 'Code of Honour' and to discipline those
who sought to break it. The culture of fear and intim-
idation this generated was such that two soldiers
murdered a code-breaker, believing that in doing so
they were fulfilling their duty to 'Unit, Corps, God
and Country'. It is easy to watch the film and be
indignant towards the system, but we should ask
whether our small or cell groups ministries have the
same potential for destruction.

Young people who are still discovering the value of
their own opinions and self-worth can be intimidated by
what appears to be an authority structure backed up by
officious job titles. Imagine the dilemma faced by a
young person who believes his/her small group is not
being properly led or, even worse, being told to do
things that make them feel uncomfortable. It is too easy
simply to expect them to challenge their leader on their
own. A small or cell groups ministry should never
become a military-style programme, thinly disguised by
friendly job titles or 'spiritual' language.

Let me make it clear: young people in small or cell
groups must always be free to challenge any statement
or request. And it is not enough merely to give them a
verbal go-ahead: they should be actively encouraged to
be critical and not simply accept everything as fact. If
this is not the case, young people become victims-in-
waiting. There need to be mechanisms in place which
enable young people to shout for help and ensure they
will be taken seriously.

I once had a very interesting discussion with a small group of fifteen-year-olds, during which I showed them a clip from the movie *Leap of Faith*. In the story, a crooked faith healer (played by Steve Martin) is exploiting and lying to a gullible crowd. Afterwards, I asked the group how they could be sure *I* wasn't, rather more subtly, doing the same to them. Their answers were both revealing and alarming. One asked, 'You wouldn't do that, would you?' Another said, 'But we *know you*.' However, none of them had ever considered on what basis they were judging me. We spent the next thirty minutes discussing what their criteria might be, with the aim that, having thought the issue through, they would be better prepared to act should the need arise. I would encourage all small-group ministries to include similar sessions in their programmes.

Practicalities

If small-group leaders are to have a respected ministry, they must be seen to be honourable in their actions. At times this will require forward planning and the ability to prevent potentially confusing situations from occurring. Before anyone can be 'taken on trust', they must first prove they are capable of being trusted by the young people, by their parents and by fellow ministry personnel. Single-sex small or cell groups are at a distinct advantage to mixed-sex groups, but they are still not immune to error.

Rather than create a complicated formula, I simply advocate that leaders think and reflect on what they already know and apply both principles and good, old fashioned common sense. For example, it is not normally appropriate for a leader to meet with a young person on his own and late at night, or to send what appear to parents to be secretive notes or coded messages. In almost all cases, any confusion can be cleared up by keeping open channels of communication. Leaders who introduce themselves to the parents of their group members, and who maintain open and regular contact, are less likely to run into trouble than those who remain distant.

Finally, it is the responsibility of all those involved in a small or cell groups ministry to highlight any area of potential confusion they become aware of. Pointing out a potentially compromising situation to a co-worker is not meddling: it is demonstrating practical support motivated by a desire to see the individual leader succeed. If this concern is not accepted as such, or the situation reoccurs, then the co-ordinator should be informed. Making yourself vulnerable and initiating a potentially difficult conversation is a small price to pay to protect the innocence of a young person and the reputation of a co-worker, the ministry and, ultimately, the faith.

Homework

- Do you know anyone who is/would be appropriately placed to provide support to the small-group leader(s) in your ministry?

Name	Telephone no.	Contacted/response

- Note down the names of five people, and state how they have made a positive contribution to your small-group ministry.

Small Group Leader	Positive contribution

- Note down five corresponding, different and creative ways that you can communicate your appreciation of the above people.

Creative affirmation	Completed

- Note down five specific questions that you believe should be asked regularly of every small-group leader.

....

....

....

....

....

7

Small groups, big peers

'One Big Mac, medium fries, regular Cola and an apple pie!' yelled the person behind the counter, and within seconds my food was being prepared. Less than a minute later, I was searching for a table, holding a tray in my hand. I sat down, took a big bite of the burger and thought, 'This is amazing!' It was not so much the quality of the burger (it was delicious!); no, it was the thought that I was eating the product of youth. The people working feverishly behind the counter were all young. Even the manager looked like his mother might still remind him to eat his McVegetables every day. There are literally tens of thousands of McDonalds restaurants all over the world, and almost all of them are staffed predominantly by young people. They successfully help run one of the world's biggest institutions.[14]

Two hundred miles south of where I was sitting, another group of people were also wearing uniforms and yelling frantic instructions at each other. They are the runners and dealers on the LIFFE floor who buy and sell tomorrow's currencies at today's prices like they were buying and selling tomatoes. Our pension funds, mortgages and other investments all rely on the demanding work performed by these young people, together with those trading shares and commodities. At an early age they are entrusted with huge responsibility and expected to do well.

Equally, young people serve in the armed forces and are expected to fight, even die, for their country. They can be given a gun before they are entitled to vote for the politicians who give the orders to use it. Still in their teens, they can be sent to Northern Ireland, Afghanistan, Iraq or anywhere else there is human conflict, and be expected to perform demanding tasks under extreme pressure.

If McDonalds, financial institutions and the armed forces are all prepared to bestow great responsibility on young people, then presumably the same will also be true of the church. Tragically, this is not the case.

> 'In 1997, Altrincham leadership seemed like just another home mission, but it wasn't.
>
> It was different in many ways – and so were those who did the leading.
>
> In Jerusalem, the average church leader was in his twenties;
> in Altrincham, he was f-f-f-forty-nine ...'
> (My adaptation of Paul Castle's hit song 'Nineteen')

Young people, with their energy, time and availability, are a gift to the church, yet it seems that they are often allowed to do little more than arrange the chairs. Sometimes I sit in meetings when names are being put forward for house group leadership, and am bemused when young people are turned down on the grounds that they are not quite ready. 'What does it take to be a leader?' I question, particularly when the young people involved are being asked to care for just a few individuals. Leading a small group is certainly not a simple task, but it is quite wrong to assume that all young people are incapable of doing it. In many cases they may perform better than older leaders.

Growing community

I have to confess that when I first started to use small or cell groups, I too assumed that the leaders would always be older people. I had never witnessed anything different. I have since seen how well some young people are able to lead small or cell groups. Of course, not every peer-led small group has worked, but then, neither has every adult-led group.

The inclusion of younger leaders requires a change in the understanding and definition of 'youth worker' and, to some extent, 'youth work'. Many people assume youth workers are always adults who do youth work *to* young people. This may benefit youth groups, but it doesn't grow community. The introduction of peer leaders changes everything. You simply end up with older leaders and younger leaders. Both have equal value and contribute towards growing community. However, for legal purposes, only those aged eighteen and over can fulfil the 'good practice' measures outlined in Chapter 5 (but not because they are any more important than those under eighteen). This change in perception is not always easy for those used to being the youth leaders. Gradually, however, the 'them' and 'us' language needs to disappear.

Benefits

There are three basic reasons why it is important to develop younger leaders. First, older leaders will benefit from the reduced pressure to recruit other, suitably skilled adults. An intentional small or cell group ministry that is growing requires a continual supply of new leaders, which even the best recruitment strategy may struggle to deliver. It is harder still when all the leaders are required to be members of one church and at least eighteen years old. In this scenario, the number of small or cell groups is soon curtailed by the availability of potential leaders, which ultimately limits the number of young people that can be served. However, create opportunities for young people to lead their own groups and suddenly the supply of potential leaders increases with every new young person added to the ministry.

Second, potential young leaders will benefit in the long-term from developing their skills. I have worked in a variety of settings. In Stourbridge I worked with excluded young people who were in and out of trouble with the police. At times, it seemed they only left town to go to prison. But on release they always came back. In Altrincham I worked with high-achieving young people who almost all went on to higher education. Few returned, preferring instead to follow the professional jobs market. For these young people, the role of youth workers was to prepare them for their future participation, wherever that might be. Yet many were leaving Altrincham ill-equipped to assume responsibilities in their new churches and Christian unions. I had to accept that the youth ministry's basic diet of energetic events, games and meaningful thoughts was simply not preparing them for Christian service. They were attending activities but not growing in their understanding or abilities. They needed opportunities to develop their gifts before they left for higher education, not afterwards, and being a small-group leader or assistant is one means of achieving this. As a result, these young people learn a range of skills that will help them both in their Christian service and future employment. Being a small-group leader requires them to set an example in their own spirituality, lifestyle and attendance; to take an active interest in and demonstrate care for other people; to communicate well; to organise activities and schedules. As a result, their confidence grows.

Gail was seventeen, and a small-group leader to six younger girls. She was doing a great job. Having been a member of a successful small group herself, she knew what was involved and was very committed to the group. The small group also had a fifteen-year-old assistant who, within a year, was able to lead a group of her own and replicate what she had learnt from Gail. Gail was always sociable, yet there was a time when she was not the keenest or most confident person. However, the support she received while in her first small group and the responsibility she was then given served her well.

The third reason why it is important to develop younger leaders is that group members benefit from having energetic, committed leaders nearer their own age who understand the purpose of small or cell groups. Young people who have benefited from being in successful small or cell groups are ideally suited to lead groups of their own. Their own personal commitment ensures that good habits are passed on to each successive generation. It was no coincidence that almost all the young people who belonged to the first small group established at Altrincham Baptist Church went on to become small-group leaders and assistants in the next cluster.

Young people sometimes perceive older leaders to be nice but essentially ignorant of the pressures faced by today's teenagers. Many an older leader has been told 'It's all right for you' or 'You don't know how hard it is'.

But the same cannot be said of younger leaders. They know exactly how hard life can be as a teenager, yet still seek to be dedicated followers of Christ and, in doing so, provide group members with credible role models. Finally, because of their comparative freedom, younger leaders have more time available for their small or cell groups and may even maintain contact with their group members while at school or college.

Involving young people in small-group leadership may sound positive, but does this mean every young person is suitable? If not, what are the necessary qualifications for a young leader?

Qualifications

Paul instructed Timothy, himself a young leader, to 'be strong in the grace that is in Christ Jesus. And the things you have heard me say in the presence of many witnesses entrust to reliable men who will also be qualified to teach others' (2 Tim. 2:1, 2). These words not only commend the development of young leaders for aspiring small-group ministries – they command it. And Timothy is not simply to grab any and every available person and charge them with the responsibility of teaching others. Instead, he should bring into leadership those he can rely on to fulfil the task properly.

Small-group leadership is a responsibility, not a right, and as such should be treated with respect. It therefore follows that not every young person will be suited to it. This may seem unfair to those who are excluded, but to fail to exclude would be damaging to all concerned. Let me explain.

First, the primary purpose of a small group is to minister to young members, not to use them as fodder in a leadership training programme. So the leader must be a capable person, irrespective of their age. Second, placing too much responsibility on someone unprepared for it sets them up for failure, damaging their confidence and potential future service. Third, just as athletes seldom achieve their personal best when a competition's entry requirements are lowered, so young people benefit from having something substantial that they can aim for. Those who have got the potential will always strive to meet the required entry level and, on doing so, gain great satisfaction from their personal development.

Requiring younger leaders to satisfy a minimum entry level demands both boldness and sensitivity, for there will be times when difficult decisions will have to be made or justified. This may be what Paul was referring to when he urged Timothy to be 'strong in the grace'. The hardest decisions occur when one close friend is included and the other is not, and where this is the case it is important that excluded individuals are reassured of their value and given the opportunity to develop.

Minimum age

The age of potential young leaders is an important factor. Too young, and they will lack the experience needed to lead others and will struggle to maintain the respect of their peers. Generally, I would expect a young leader to be at least sixteen years old, and an assistant to be about a year younger than that. They then have enough time to develop as group members and to appreciate the benefits of being in the group, yet still have two years left in which to lead.

Young people are often better suited to leading same-sex small or cell groups that consist of still younger members. A sixteen-year-old leader can have a significant impact on a group of fourteen-year-olds but may struggle to lead a group of their own age effectively. In the latter instance, all but the most exceptional young leaders find it difficult to redefine the relationship with their peers and, as a result, tend to be either too overbearing or too lackadaisical.

Defining moment

For young leaders to serve with integrity and conviction, I would expect them to have made a public declaration of faith, be that baptism or confirmation, and for that to have been a defining moment in their own spiritual journey. In effect, by choosing to make this stand, they draw a line under their childlike ways and demonstrate a desire to be dedicated followers of Christ. It is precisely because this is such a challenging step that I believe it serves as a good indicator of leadership potential. The same requirement would not necessarily be expected of an assistant, but experience shows that most do go on to be baptised or confirmed. Often the period spent serving as an assistant helps to clarify the young person's desire to be a dedicated follower of Christ.

Adam was a very unassuming sixteen-year-old who became an assistant leader to a seventeen-year-old small-group leader. He became one of the prime 'movers and shakers' in the youth ministry. His first action was to organise a trip to watch a floodlit match at the nearby Lancashire County Cricket Club – not a bad way to start a ministry with sports-mad lads. Adam's 'defining moment' came when he decided to be baptised. Prior to this, he had given little indication of where he stood, one way or the other. However, during the baptismal classes he demonstrated a tried-and-tested faith and a real desire to serve

God. It was thrilling to hear him say, in front of hundreds of people, that he wanted to be a dedicated follower of Christ. Those in his small group witnessed Adam's 'defining moment' and were in no doubt that when he spoke of spiritual things he did so with integrity.

Servant attitude

Some young people may fulfil the above criteria but still not be suitable for small-group leadership because they appear to be seeking status rather than service. Becoming a leader should never be regarded as a reward for good conduct or a sign of special favour but, rather, a demonstration of a commitment to serve sacrificially the needs of others. Young leaders can sometimes misunderstand the significance of this and will need constant reminding of Jesus' challenge: 'If anyone wants to be first, he must be the very last, and the servant of all' (Mk. 9:35). If the essential trust between young members and leaders is to be maintained, there can be no room for inflated egos or oppressive leadership, no matter how 'gifted' the individual may be.

Young leaders should be some of the most hard-working ministry members, always prepared to be the first to arrive and the last to leave. Those who are lazy and work-shy are unlikely to change as a consequence of becoming leaders. A good indication of a person's leadership potential is their willingness to find jobs that need doing and to get on with them.

Making it work

Being a small-group leader is always demanding, but being a younger leader is harder still. Those who seek to serve in this capacity deserve to be supported every step of the way. Young leaders can be set up to fail through being given too much responsibility too soon and receiving too little support too late. Adopting the following simple measures can make all the difference between success and failure.

Mentoring

A posse of young leaders came to see me a few months after they were appointed, and told me of their frustration at not knowing what to do or who to ask. They felt alone, vulnerable and were beginning to doubt the usefulness of their ministry. Nonetheless, they were still keen to serve. I apologised for not having provided them with the support they deserved. The next step was to demonstrate that I had recognised their situation. With their number increasing, it became clear that looking after young leaders was becoming a job in itself, so an older leader was set aside to develop them. This person had the satisfying task of meeting regularly with the younger leaders, both on their own and collectively, and equipping them in their spirituality and service. Such mentoring should be an enriching experience for younger and older leader alike as they seek to learn from each other's experiences and insight.

Directing an older leader to such a task might appear a luxury not all youth ministries can afford, but it is not as extravagant as it sounds. The involvement of the younger leaders could potentially render the older ones redundant, enabling them to concentrate on troubleshooting and leadership development. By becoming a leader of leaders, each older person is then able to support up to five small or cell groups. This demonstrates responsible stewardship, not extravagance.

Partnerships

When I was seventeen, I spent a number of weeks touring remote parts of India, often spending considerable periods of time alone. Having to deal with such an unfamiliar environment on my own became, at times, almost intolerable. Looking back, I can see that if I had had a travelling companion I would have been far better able to deal with the problems I came up against. In the same way, younger leaders often benefit from working in pairs, which enables them to support one another in an unfamiliar role. They should be encouraged to pray together regularly, both for each other and for their groups, and to discuss what they believe to be the groups' needs. In this way, their partnership becomes real and God-centred.

Often when a small group is led by a young person, the distinction between leader and assistant becomes blurred. This is healthy and should be encouraged. In partnership, it is not uncommon for one eventually to overshadow the other. Whilst this may not at first be an issue, there can come a time when the needs of both are best served if they work separately. Gail brought her best friend, Andrea, to the youth programme and they became dedicated followers of Christ. They went everywhere together and were soon both in leadership roles. Yet it was always Gail who took the lead. At first Andrea benefited greatly from this, but eventually it became clear that her reliance on Gail was preventing her from developing her own potential. With their agreement, they were assigned to different small or cell groups and the result was very positive for both.

Framework

Young leaders need the security of a strong framework. They rarely have sufficient experience or confidence to design their own programmes and so must rely on the provision of suitable material. Those who support young leaders must have both a working knowledge of their groups and access to a range of suitable resources.

The cell-group model places particular emphasis on developing young leaders, so the accompanying resources can sometimes appear as prescriptive as a McDonalds system in their attention to detail and conformity. Indeed, the pack produced by American-based High Impact Ministries[15] seems, at first, to be almost claustrophobic in its prescriptive detail, until you appreciate the intended young age of the cell-group leaders. Where this is the case, checklists, forms and prescribed session plans can all be reassuring to young leaders and those who seek to manage them.

Young leaders may not at first inspire the full confidence of their small-group members and parents, but this should not last. Potential difficulties can often be lessened by introducing the older leader who is supporting the younger one, to group members and parents, and reassuring them of their ongoing accessibility. In doing so, care should be taken not to undermine the younger leader's position.

Giving young people meaningful responsibility is an undeniable risk, but it is one that is usually worth taking. There will be times when a young leader makes a mistake or experiences a crisis of confidence, and it is then they will need to know that someone will be there to catch them, should they fall. There may be occasions when a young leader does something foolish and has to withdraw, but this should not be used as an excuse to deny all young people leadership responsibilities. There are potentially great rewards to be had for small or cell groups ministries which have the courage and the vision to develop the leadership skills of their young people.

Homework

- Which of the young people in your care do you believe
  are potential small-group leaders or assistants?

....

....

....

....

- Who is the most appropriate person to support these
  young leaders? How will this be achieved?

....

....

....

....

Part 2

LEADING GROUPS

8

Small groups, big dynamics

Hollywood has always been fascinated by human tragedy, but the 1970s in particular seemed to produce a bumper harvest of disaster movies. Planes crashed, buildings burnt, dams burst, ocean liners sank, cable-cars jammed and earthquakes shook. Disaster-prone individuals turned up in the wrong place at the wrong time. Special-effects technicians were in celluloid heaven as scenic panoramas were dropped in favour of relentless crashes and mind-blowing explosions.

Yet it was the scriptwriters who managed to create the real drama. It was not enough to be trapped inside a damaged cable-car high up a remote mountainside with little prospect of living long enough to spend the holiday insurance – this had to be done in the company of one's fellow-passengers. Moreover, all the passengers had to have very different temperaments and personalities, causing emotional sparks to fly with every new explosion. Part of the fun in watching these films was to identify the characters and predict what role they would play in the group.

Believing they were all going to die, *Joker* would sit in the corner clutching a bottle of whisky and cracking terrible jokes. *Negative* was essentially a coward who rejected all escape plans and violently clashed with their source, *Captain Sensible*. After an hour, *Martyr* would sign his own death certificate by revealing a shameful secret which inevitably meant he had to be killed while performing some remarkably daring but suicidal feat. Taking charge of the group would be *Reluctant Hero* who, incidentally, was always male. He would be the one who calmed the group and brought about their dramatic rescue, ably assisted by his female lead, *Miss Unflappable* (with the fluttering eyelashes and torn, flowing dress). After ninety minutes, all but *Martyr* would emerge to live to see another disaster. Having survived a cable-car disaster, some had the tragic misfortune to find themselves in an horrific train crash just months later. How unfair was that?

At times it seems there is another disaster movie in the making – 'Small Group 2003'. It may not require dramatic special effects, but it would give scriptwriters a similar opportunity to explore characters and their interpersonal relationships. How will the disparate assortment of individuals cope with being trapped together in a submerged small group? When all other small or cell groups resemble perfect examples of fun and supportive communities, why is it only yours that appears to be crumbling? The young people may be long-term friends, but put them in a small group and they can seem intent on destroying one another. Soon even making coffee after the service can appear more appealing than having to tame this wild bunch.

If you are experiencing thoughts like these, take a deep breath, go make yourself a hot drink, and read on. In this chapter we will look at how group dynamics affect small or cell groups.

Group roles

All groups contain people with varying temperaments and personalities. Part of the challenge of leading a group is understanding the roles each person plays, for only then will you be able to serve them adequately.

Let's imagine a group of eight young people. Each plays a defined role, and the leader's task is to bring them together so that they form a community. In meeting these imaginary members, you should be able to recognise some of your own young people and hopefully understand them better. Because all groups are different, there will inevitably be some differences between your actual small group and this imaginary one. First, not all the roles are found in all groups. Second some young people have the ability to play more than one role, so you may need to combine two or more roles to form one actual personality. This said, let me introduce you to eight personalities who, together, form Spud's small group.

Dominator

The first person to stand out in the group is *Dominator*. He always manages to be the centre of attention. If someone has a question, he has an answer. When someone makes a statement, he cuts in with his own, often unrelated, utterance. He has 'been there and done that' before anyone else has even thought about it. His voice is loud and his body language louder still. In short, he is one hell of a guy. If only *Dominator* would listen to what others have to say.

Yet many a group comes into existence as a result of *Dominator* inviting his entourage to participate. His presence gives value to the other members who like to be associated with such confident people.

Spectator

At the opposite end of the room and seated closest to the exit is *Spectator*. He is content to watch what the rest of the group is doing. Only a mind-reader could know whether his silence is a result of profound boredom, intense interest or an inability to make himself heard. He never contributes to a discussion, and direct questions receive a minimal response. If only *Spectator* would say something.

Yet Spectator may simply be deciding if this is a safe group to join. Alternatively, he may be sufficiently secure in his own beliefs not always to have the last word. He is content to let others go first.

Gladiator

Gladiator loves to fight; it doesn't matter who it's with or what it's about. In a heated debate, she can easily become frustrated by her inability to win a point or express herself adequately. She often feels threatened by those she perceives to be superior to herself and, when cornered, she lashes out. She deals with this by running away, either physically or emotionally, and seeking solitude. If only *Gladiator* would take a deep breath and get a grip on her emotions.

That said, *Gladiator* is good at standing up for people, and will often be fiercely loyal to those who are vulnerable. In a hostile world, she can be a comforting presence.

Placator

Running around after *Gladiator* is *Placator*. She hates conflict and will do everything possible to ensure nothing is ever 'said'. She prefers to sweep things under the carpet rather than deal with them in the open. She can appear anxious and often overly concerned that the group will fall apart. If only Placator would say what she really thinks.

Nevertheless, *Placator* is very good at uniting the group; after all, someone needs to keep the peace. She is very sensitive to other people's feelings and is a good listener.

Motivator

Motivator is an idealist in need of a cause. Individuals take second place as he pushes on towards his goal. Sitting down to discuss endless questions is a waste of time – there is real work to be done. *Motivator* can appear somewhat pious and intimidate the rest of the group (not to mention the group leader). If only *Motivator* would stop being so perfect.

However, it is *Motivator* who often reminds the group about those who have yet to join them. He is also usually the one most able to articulate where the group is going.

Terminator

Faced with such optimism, *Terminator* takes it upon himself to lend a touch of realism. Positive suggestions are met with ten reasons why they won't work. His pessimism and disinterest can dampen the enthusiasm of newcomers. He doesn't even have to speak; his body language says it all. If only *Terminator* would think positively.

But *Terminator* may sometimes be right. Not every idea is appropriate, and even good ones have flaws. By identifying problems, he ensures that others can solve them.

Orator

Just when a discussion gets interesting, *Orator* diverts attention with an unrelated statement or question. Not only that, she doesn't know when to stop talking. Running out of intelligent things to say doesn't seem to make a difference. When she gets going, everyone else gives up. She has a theory about almost everything and even an opinion about opinionated people. If only *Orator* would stop talking.

Yet, whenever there is an awkward silence, *Orator* gets a discussion going. She is often able to introduce lateral or 'deeper' thoughts, to the benefit of the rest of the group.

Actor

All the world's a stage for *Actor* as she seeks the affirmation of her latest audience. One minute she can be playing the 'funny' part, next it's the 'straight' role, but rarely will she accept a walk-on part. A passionate being, she is either 'up' or 'down', never in between. When the atmosphere becomes too intense or challenging, she soon diverts attention with a quick gag and prevents the conversation from getting any deeper. If only Actor would be herself.

Actor is great fun to be with and adept at helping others to feel relaxed, particularly those who don't want to take centre stage themselves.

Group understanding

Recognising the different roles people play in small or cell groups is an important step towards growing community. In describing these personalities, I have tried to include both the positive and negative contributions they make to group life, the two sides of the coin. People's weaknesses are often their strengths, and *vice versa*. Someone may be good at imagining what could be achieved tomorrow, but poor at dealing with detail today. You will serve a young person best when, recognising the positive, you help them to recognise the negative. If you react against the negative, you may repress the positive, which would be self-defeating. Considerable amounts of understanding and self-control are required!

Being aware of your own values and how they influence your perspective on life is also important. What you consider to be negative others may believe to be positive. You may judge an act to be rebellion, but others might interpret it as a God-given opportunity to challenge and create. After all, the Bible and church history are full of 'rebellious' people who achieved great things for God.

Bringing group members on in this way will be possible only if you are willing to get to know each young person and invest time in them. Small or cell groups which are programme-driven, and which only function during formal sessions, will struggle to develop this level of understanding and so miss an important component of community. There is no substitute for sitting down with one or two young people and just talking. And be prepared for conversations to be challenging for you as well as the young people.

Group tools

Most small or cell groups involve some semi-formal sessions that provide an opportunity for the group members and the leader to work together on a particular issue or project. The presence of the various group roles, however, can sometimes make these gatherings difficult. Careful use of the following simple measures could make all the difference.

Affirmation

Often with young – and not-so-young – people, difficult behaviour arises out of a lack of self-worth. *Orator* may talk incessantly because she is seeking praise for her 'worthy' contribution; *Gladiator* may defend the weak because she wants to feel needed; *Spectator* may opt out, believing that others are always better than him. All these personalities would benefit from positive and consistent affirmation. So great care needs to be taken when someone gives what the rest of the group believes to be a 'wrong' answer. It should be possible to disagree with a statement but still affirm the contribution of each individual.

Body language

Every gesture we make communicates something. The way you stand, what you do with your hands and where you look all help to tell a story. An awareness of body language will enable you to manage the signals you send to others and interpret those they are sending back to you. If you keep glancing at the clock, doodling on a pad or yawning, you will communicate a lack of interest to the group. Similarly, two young people creating some sort of diversion is often an indication that they have had enough and it's time for the group to do something different.

More intentionally, body language can be used to include new people in a discussion and, if necessary,

exclude others. If Dominator is not giving others sufficient room to participate, make direct eye contact with
him, then deliberately move your focus to Spectator. If
necessary, repeat this process until both recognise that a
change of contributor is expected. Some young people
find joining a discussion difficult and so you may need
to draw them in by throwing them a verbal lifeline. 'So,
Spectator, what do you think?' Conversely, by physically leaning back or turning away from someone, you
can slow them down.

Questions

Sometimes questions may be used either to include
Spectator or restrain *Orator*, both of whom may be going
in different directions to the rest of the group. Questions
should be clear and designed to confirm what people
know rather than expose what they don't. For this reason, rhetorical or impossibly challenging questions are
unhelpful. If in doubt, only ask a question when you
know the group has a realistic chance of providing the
answer.

Well-crafted questions can have a profound effect on
a small group, but not all questions are constructed so
well. To test this, try answering the following two questions and decide which of them is the better one:

- 'Does anyone here watch TV?'

- '*Placator*, why do you watch TV?'

The first question only allows for a Yes/No response
and does not stimulate discussion. Neither is it targeted
at a specific individual, so the whole group may choose
not to answer it. However, the second is much better.

Placator is in no doubt who is expected to provide an answer and has to state her personal opinion, not just the facts. The detail she gives provides further opportunity to ask the all-important supplementary questions that either *Placator* or other group members might have. Skilled interviewers usually manage to draw others into the discussion so that it becomes multi-directional rather than uni-directional. Listen to the types of questions asked in television debates and news interviews, and see what you can learn from them.

Seating

Where people are seated in relation to each other can influence the dynamics of a small group. For example, if *Gladiator* is spoiling for a fight, the best way to deal with the situation may be to sit immediately next to her where subtle use of body language can both reassure and restrain. If the leader sits opposite her, the dynamic becomes combative – they resemble fighters in opposite corners of a ring. In fact, the person the leader ought to be sitting opposite is Spectator, or anyone else who needs encouragement to join a conversation. Then body language can be used to bring them in.

Most rooms provide an obvious focal point, and whoever occupies this space is often assumed to be the one in control. If your intention as leader is to facilitate rather than control the group, it is advisable for you to sit elsewhere. If there aren't enough chairs, make sure you are the one who sits on the floor, as height often equates with power. Remember the importance of eye contact and make sure everyone is within winking distance of each other. If necessary, invite those on the fringe to move in.

Direct intervention

There will be times when *Dominator* and *Orator* do not respond to subtle interventions and, for the sake of the whole group, you will need to take more decisive action. This should not be because you need to reassert authority, but rather because all else has failed. Try applying all the above measures in one sweeping action, saying something like, 'David, thank you for your contribution. I appreciate all you have to say, and can we now open up the discussion? Maria, what do you think ...?' As you do so, lean away from David and towards Maria, using your hands to gently direct the discussion traffic. If necessary, repeat this at a later point in the session. Incidentally, notice how 'and' is far more constructive than 'but'. If you haven't, try re-reading the above sentence using 'but' instead of 'and'.

In seeking to encourage Maria, you should make sure David is not totally deflated. As soon as the session ends, reassure him of your support. Direct intervention may have solved the immediate needs of the wider group, but it is unlikely to have had much positive effect on him. It may be appropriate to arrange a further opportunity to discuss what happened, and this may be your chance to help David come to his own conclusions about what went wrong.

Group leaders

Small-group leaders have great influence on their small-group members, and how they perceive 'leadership' can determine the inner workings of their groups. A leader who expects to be the centre of the group, with members seated around them, will set a very different tone to the one who imagines the leader's place as being on the outside looking in. By giving thought to appropriate leadership styles, a leader should be able to engineer the dynamics of the group.

It seems most leaders continue the pattern set by their own leaders, past or present. This allows both good and bad habits to be passed on to successive generations, and it is important that all leaders spend time regularly reflecting on what they believe to be helpful practice in their ministries.

As before with the group roles, let's look at five leadership styles and see how relevant they are to your current practice.

Dictator: 'You listen; I make the decisions'

Dictator takes control of the group because he knows what is best for it. He doesn't waste time asking people what they think because he already knows the answer. It is he who determines what the group will do, when and where. He asks the questions and sets the answers but, in reality, he spends more time making statements. As leader, he retains total control of the group.

Negotiator: 'I listen; I make the decisions'

Negotiator recognises he is responsible for the group and is prepared to make the difficult decisions. However, he is keen for group members to influence him. He asks questions because he is genuinely interested in what people have to say. He will sometimes let the group make a decision for themselves, but only on minor matters. As leader, he negotiates with those less powerful than himself.

Participator: 'We listen; we make the decisions'

Participator considers herself a member of the group. Decisions are made collectively, with everyone given equal opportunity to influence the final outcome. Responsibility is shared equally between all members, and it is at this level that she contributes. She does not control the agenda, and group members are free to ask questions of anyone about anything. They may choose to recognise her as their leader but are always free to change their minds. As leader, she is an equal stake-holder.

Facilitator: 'We listen; you make the decisions'

Facilitator aims to serve the group, of which she is not an equal member. The group members are responsible for directing their own affairs, and her charge is to help them be self-sufficient. As someone slightly detached from the group she brings suggestions and occasionally an alternative perspective, but she is careful not to impose her own values. As leader, she is a less-than-equal adviser.

Spectator: 'I listen; you make the decisions'

At the opposite end of the spectrum is *Spectator*. His presence may provide some initial reassurance, but the group is not reliant upon him. They make all their own decisions, leaving him to observe – but not interfere. As leader, he has no need for power.

Despite many pretenders, you will not find a book that offers the perfect leadership style, because each small group requires a unique approach. All the above styles are, depending on the context, both right and wrong. In practice, most small or cell groups require their leader to be flexible enough to deliver different styles at different times. The early stages of a small group cycle usually require a more directive approach, but, as group members develop, this may become too restrictive.

Small-group leaders should always aim for their members to be self-determining at the earliest opportunity. This means providing increasing opportunities for shared responsibility and supporting them in their learning process. The cell group-model is particularly good at emphasising the servant nature of leaders and the need for them to be facilitators.

Homework

- Reflect on the young people you are currently working with, and consider the positive and negative contributions they make to small group life. What, if any, action should you take?

Name: ....

Positive: ....

Negative: ....

Action: ....

Name: ....

Positive: ....

Negative: ....

Action: ....

Name: ....

Positive: ....

Negative: ....

Action: ....

Name: ....

Positive: ....

Negative: ....

Action: ....

Name: ....

Positive: ....

Negative: ....

Action: ....

- Reflect on your own recent leadership experiences, and record examples which demonstrate the five different leadership styles:

Dictator: ....

Negotiator: ....

Participator: ....

Facilitator: ....

Spectator: ....

9

Small groups, big community

I took off my heavy rucksack and sank to the ground, exhausted by the day's expedition. The terrain had been severe and the heat intense. Now I needed to eat. A quick hunt through my pack revealed what was on the menu for today – dehydrated beef-and-onion mince. Without stopping to read the instructions, I boiled some water, opened the silver packet and sprinkled in the space-age contents. A chemical reaction almost immediately thickened the mixture of dust and water, causing violent bubbles and strange smells to he emitted into the mountain air. As soon as hunger told me the gourmet meal was cooked, I began to eat. A TV chef creation could not have tasted better. It was slightly crunchy but very filling. When I'd finished eating, I had an incredible thirst and drank a large quantity of water.

Soon I began to feel somewhat peculiar – as though I'd swallowed a balloon that was now inflating slowly inside my stomach. It transpired that I had not used enough water when cooking the dehydrated meal. Now, another chemical reaction – this time inside my stomach – was making my after-dinner drink expand the meal still further. Once again, violent bubbles and strange smells were emitted into the mountain air. I had been so keen to satisfy my hunger, I had not allowed sufficient time for the meal's preparation and, as a result, was left feeling very uncomfortable. I rolled around the mountains waiting for nature to take its course. What had taken just two minutes to prepare, and even less to eat, took three days to leave! This tale of mountain misery holds a lesson for those who lead small or cell groups.

Small or cell groups ministries may have the potential to satisfy young people's hunger for community, but they can only achieve this when the right ingredients are given sufficient time and space to simmer. Simply throwing the human contents of a small group together and expecting instant 'community' is unrealistic. The real thing can only be achieved with patience, commitment and a dash of imagination.

Growing community is a process requiring careful and deliberate action, in which the journey becomes as important as the destination.

Understanding community

Community is one of those words that is frequently used but rarely understood. For some, it denotes a geographical neighbourhood or village; for others, it points to the egalitarian aspiration of a new world order; or it conjures up the image of the 'hippie' commune of people who choose to live together as an extended family. But, for the Christian, there is a spiritual dimension to community. Please hang on in here as we go a little deeper for a few minutes.

God may be one (Dt. 6:4) but is also three persons – Father, Son and Holy Spirit – who coexist perfectly and eternally. This three-in-oneness (which is what the doctrine of the trinity is all about) reveals the community that lies at the heart of God's very being. This is clearly illustrated at Jesus' baptism, where all three persons of the trinity interact with each other, performing different tasks whilst still supporting one another: God the Son receives the affirmation of God the Father and the indwelling of God the Spirit (Mt. 3:16, 17; Lk. 3:21, 22). God isn't just an advocate of community: he is community; it is part of his nature.

God said, 'Let us make man in our image, in our likeness ...' (Gen. 1:26, 27; 2:7, 18, 20–24). He created Adam and Eve and ensured both bore the characteristics of his nature. This account from Genesis does more than just legitimise marriage; it describes a basic, human, God-given design for community. In short, people need each other.

'God blessed them and said to them, "Be fruitful and increase in number; fill the earth and subdue it. ..."' (Gen.1:28). Those who are made in his image are to share in the enterprise of creating an authentic community. Those who are renewed in Christ are to participate in the divine nature (2 Pet.1:4).

> God is love. Whoever lives in love lives in God, and God in him. In this way, love is made complete among us so that we will have confidence on the day of judgment, because in this world we are like him.
>
> 1 Jn. 4:16, 17

We express our community on earth by linking into the community in heaven. God and his people become connected as heaven and earth are brought together to create a community that extends beyond the boundaries of time and space.

This understanding of community is based, not primarily on our behaviour or our attitudes toward one another, but on our acceptance of Christ. It is only through him that we gain access to the Father (Jn. 14:9) and to the Spirit (Jn. 14:26). Consequently, without Christ there can be no authentic community, for he says, '[For] where two or three come together in my name, there am I with them' (Mt. 18:20). In its most basic form, growing community means drawing people into Christ-centred 'togetherness', encompassing all that is done in his name. Community is at the heart of the church and she engages in fellowship, worship, mission and discipleship. Community is definitely a spiritual matter.

Stages of community

Though instant community is not achievable, it is possible to identify a number of stages in the process of community development. Most group development theories rely on their groups having a definite beginning and an end. All the members join at the same time and share the same experiences. However, in reality, small or cell groups are much more fluid than this, and any attempt to understand the process of development must allow for members to come and go at different points in time. This is particularly important for small or cell groups that comprise young people and exist to attract new members. So rather than asking what stage the whole group is at, I find it more helpful to determine where each member is in the process.

Now let me identify what I believe are the five stages of group development necessary in growing community. On the basis that to take an idea from one person is plagiarism, but to quote the idea of many is research, I have been helped by what others have categorised as 'Forming', 'Storming', 'Norming' and 'Performing'.[16]

Start up

In this first stage of the process, a prospective small or cell group member comes into contact with existing members and makes a judgment based on what she sees. The prospective member needs reassuring that the community is genuinely welcoming, caring and, above all, dynamic. It is here that social activities come into their own. Remember, two's company, three's an evangelistic barbecue! During this time, the prospective member is considering if she really wants to join the group and, if the answer is 'Yes', how this is done. Often the primary consideration is who else is in the group and whether she will gain anything from being associated with it. In asking hard questions – whether vocalised or not – the potential member is saying, 'Tell me why I should belong.'

However, some prospective members don't join because they are never invited to the group or, if they are, made to feel sufficiently welcome by the group members.

Sign up

Once a prospective member has decided to join, she becomes a novice member. She soon begins to discover what it takes to belong. The novice determines what behaviour is required, who plays what role and how the group operates. She needs help and encouragement to fit in with the rest of the group, and reassurance that she is accepted by them. She will often voluntarily adopt recognisable signs of solidarity, which might include a similar dress code, language, behaviour or even choice of music. During this stage the novice is, in effect, inducted into the community by the other members who tolerate her lack of understanding. The provision of 'just looking' programmes, like the Alpha Course, can be very effective at this point. As she asks searching questions, the novice is saying, 'Tell me what I should do or be like to belong.'

Yet, some novices leave at this point because they cannot accept the group's practices or beliefs, or because the community does not live up to their expectations.

Stick up

Now that the novice feels secure within the small or cell group community, she becomes more critical, questioning some of the long-accepted 'group-speak' that is passed on from the other members. This includes asking fundamental questions, such as why people adopt certain roles, who gets to make the decisions, and how successful is the group in fulfilling its purpose. This can cause conflict with other group members who feel threatened by this challenge to the status quo. Nevertheless, the critic's contribution provides significant 'added value' to the group and ensures that it continues to evolve. The critic needs to be able to ask these awkward questions and to think the unimaginable – while still receiving acceptance and appreciation. The small-group leader may play the role of mediator. As she asks penetrating questions, the critic is saying, 'Tell me why, in order to belong, I should still believe and do what you say?'

However, some leave during this stage because conflict within the group remains unresolved.

Stand up

Coming out of the critical stage, the young person becomes an established member and begins to accept some responsibility for others in the group, and thus relieve the leader of some tasks. This is the first time the established member is able to take a genuine interest in others who are at different stages from herself. She needs encouragement to develop her skills and to take her place within the community.

Where this does not happen, she may well revert to the critical stage. Encouragement involves letting her participate in group activities, inviting and welcoming potential members, inducting novices and wrestling with critics. As she seeks to establish her role, she is asking, 'Tell me where I can serve?'

At this stage, some leave to start new groups of their own and yet others may drop out because they are unwilling to shoulder extra responsibility.

Shut up

In most cases, winding up a small or cell group should be a positive step as it provides an opportunity to celebrate the success of its young members in growing the group. Remember, intentional small-group ministries are those that grow and multiply, and every group member should be aiming for the day when their group becomes two. Some fixed-term small or cell groups, such as those associated with the Alpha Course, may have a short shelf-life. There are, however, some occasions when a group will require winding up for less positive reasons. Those that do not grow at all should, after a year, be examined for fatal flaws such as poor leadership, lack of vision, low morale, emotionally demanding members or de-motivating sessions. Group members should be encouraged to determine their own solutions but, if the purpose is to be a growing community, then an executive decision may be required to restart the group. Community is not fostered when a struggling group is left to flounder.

Community values

For growing community to move from rhetoric to reality, commitment is required from both the leader and the group. A first constructive step would be for the group to determine its own way of operating and the values it holds to be important. One way to achieve this would be for them to design their own contract together; a contract encompasses a mix of idealism and realism, which everyone is then asked to sign. In doing this, the group members and the leader are pledging their support for one another. To ensure that values are genuinely owned and understood by the group, someone with access to a computer should be responsible for producing a final document for every member to keep. To take in new members, draw up a fresh contract at the start of each ministry year.

In establishing the contract, the leaders should never impose own values on a reluctant group, but instead should be prepared to use well-crafted questions that encourage the young people to reflect on issues they may have overlooked. Listed below are some of the most basic community values.

Acceptance

On joining a small or cell group, one of the big questions a young person will have is 'Am I safe?' If they feel they are not, it is highly unlikely they will choose to share anything of personal value with the group. The group needs to create an environment in which everyone, including the leader, is free to be themselves. So, what happens if one member admits to a belief or an action that is not shared by the others? Very often group members will detect and imitate the response of the leader, so it is important that the leader demonstrates total acceptance at all times. Acceptance requires the group to tolerate those who are different.

Confidentiality

It should never be assumed that group members appreciate the meaning or are even aware of the existence of group confidentiality. Leaders should frequently remind them that nothing said in a session should be passed on to someone outside the group. The only exception would be where an individual is understood to be 'at risk'. In these circumstances, the leader has both a legal and a moral obligation to inform the relevant authority. However, this should not be done in a secretive manner.

Honesty

Having tested the reliability of the group's acceptance and confidentiality, the young people will need encouragement to make full use of the supportive small group environment. Very few people find this a natural thing to do, and the leader may need to initiate this by setting a personal example. I have often found that a reluctant group will only begin to share matters of personal significance with each other as a result of something I have first said to them. A leader who leads with trivia will reap a trivial response.

Conflict

I hate confrontation and will do anything to avoid or ignore it, but I have to concede that I am restricting the growth of community by doing this. Conflict, like anger (Eph. 4:26), can bring people together and help them deal with personal issues. All groups will experience conflict at some stage in their development and, because it can be used constructively, leaders should not panic when it occurs. Very often, supporting young people in conflict results in significant personal development. Skilful leaders will be able to help them question their own presuppositions and values without taking sides. An important part of the process is the need to practice forgiveness; without this there will be no satisfactory resolution to conflict.

Community builders

There are a number of practical measures, which are neither complicated nor costly, that small-group leaders can employ to transform their groups from collections of individuals to authentic communities.

Identity

Small or cell groups of young people aged eleven to fourteen often benefit from adopting self-styled identities for their small or cell groups. Pop groups, sports teams and an unlimited assortment of peculiar names can be called on to create a sense of identity and belonging. This may introduce constructive competition and healthy rivalry between groups. The resulting energy and commitment often leads to the growth and subsequent multiplication of small or cell groups.

Socials

Small or cell groups which only ever sit in circles, discussing 'deep' issues, soon become squares, so it is important to provide the young people with opportunities to socialise and get to know each other. It is a myth to label social activities as 'worldly' prerequisites to real ministry: a healthy social calendar is as much ministry as anything else. The group aim is to minister to the whole person, catering for people's physical, social, intellectual, emotional and spiritual needs.

One of the youth leaders I know took a small group of young males on an overnight canoeing trip. Two years later, they were still talking about it. Most social activities will be far less demanding – eating pizza, playing a game, watching a match, hosting a surprise party for someone. But give careful thought to the financial resources of each young person: you won't be growing community by forcing some members to miss out on activities they can't afford. The group should be expected to generate their own ideas and to make any necessary arrangements, leaving the leader to support them in the process. A relaxed environment will encourage conversation and allow a young person to bring up a concern or ask questions. A range of possible social activities is outlined in Part 3.

Informal time

Small-group leaders should never be perceived as spiritual 'doctors', only seen when necessity demands it. An intentional small or cell group ministry should not be a smaller version of a youth group, meeting only at a fixed time to discuss a fixed agenda. Proponents of the cell model rightly stress the importance of putting people before programmes, and warn against a curriculum-driven approach. One way to combat this is to encourage group members to meet together at unscheduled times, and leaders could create opportunities to meet with them in between formal sessions. This might involve occasionally inviting them round for a meal, helping out with a project or going on a walk together. Leaders who make themselves available to their group usually achieve far more than those who restrict personal encounters to formal sessions only.

Cards, calls and e-mails

Since young people tend to receive far less mail than their parents, cards sent in the post are often well received. As well as at Christmas and on birthdays, you can send cards to congratulate people on a well-played match, successful exam results, the best joke cracked at the last group session ... After a difficult day at school or college, coming home to find a card from someone saying they are thinking of you can be very encouraging. The phenomenal rise in text messaging, as well as use of e-mail, provides another simple means of maintaining informal contact with group members.

Food

I do not think it a coincidence that Jesus spent so much of his time sharing meals with people. It is during informal occasions like these that relationships are built and values shared.[17] One of the reasons for the success of the Alpha Course, I believe, is its use of meals – participants are able to relax and get to know each other. Though at first it may be helpful for the leader to provide the food, eventually each person could join in by bringing something. Eating together confirms the importance of each individual and is a simple means of demonstrating community. Even sessions that include more formal discussion could benefit from organising a group meal. After all, this is precisely what happened at what was to be the last meeting of Jesus' small group (Mt. 26:17–30).

Service projects

There is something powerful about a group of young people working together for the benefit of others. There is always a danger that groups become inward-focused and narrow. Working hard to provide for the needs of others may be a positive antidote, so it is very healthy for a small group to take on a service project such as: regularly visiting a residential care home; transforming someone's garden; painting a church room; or raising both awareness and money for a world issue. An effective way to introduce this approach is to participate in a structured programme such as that offered by Oasis Youth Action. Spending a week in an unfamiliar environment brings the group together and enables them to learn principles that they can then implement when back at home. Some groups 'adopt a child' through organisations such as Tearfund and encourage their members to contribute financially towards the costs. Relating to a young person from a totally different country and culture enhances the group's sense of community. However, when considering this option, it is important to stress the long-term and consistent commitment required by the sponsoring members.

Vision

Finally, there is a continual need to remind group members (and leaders) of the inherent value of becoming a growing community. By 'talking it up', small-group leaders will enable young people to see the group's potential and their own individual roles within it. There may be occasions when a leader is required to challenge an attitude or action, which weakens the group's sense of community. Where this happens, a full explanation should always be given and the individual(s) helped to make a more positive contribution.

Finally ...

Community may seem like a dream that most aspire to, but with hard work and imagination it can become reality. At times, this may be difficult to imagine and even harder to describe, but there is nothing more rewarding than seeing an assortment of young people transformed into a growing community. Small-group ministries are ideally equipped to achieve this, and very often it is the quality of group life that attracts potential members to sign up. Growing community leads, not only to relational but also numerical growth, with a direct correlation between the growth in the quality of relationships and the quantity of members. How to see numerical growth in a small-group ministry will be explored in the next chapter.

Homework

- Take a moment to dream a little. Describe what you believe community would be like in the ideal young person's small group.

....

....

....

....

....

Use this as a basis for prayer and ask God to make this dream come true.

- List five practical measures, not already mentioned, which you could employ to grow community within your group of young people.

....

....

....

....

....

10

Small groups, big growth

The car was perfectly parked in a quiet road, securely locked and facing the right direction. Apart from the odd spot of rust and an aversion to hills, there was nothing wrong with it. A few hours later, however, a big dent had appeared in the front nearside wheel-arch. Someone had obviously crashed into it and not stopped to confess. The car looked in a sorry state but was still just about drivable and so, once I had stopped breathing out murderous threats, off I went. However, after a few miles I began to feel a strain in my left arm. The damaged wheel-arch was causing the car to pull to the left; if I let go of the steering-wheel, the car would swerve off the road. To compensate for this tendency towards self-destruction, I had to use extra strength to pull the steering-wheel back to where it should be. It soon became clear that some repair work was urgently needed.

All small-group ministries seem to have similar in-built self-destruct mechanisms that – unless corrected – pulls them off course. What begin as vibrant, healthy and out-ward-focused groups can become self-centred, lethargic and inward-looking. It is ironic that the attributes of authentic community, which once attracted new people, can easily lead to the formation of an exclusive club in which members settle for what they can get out of the group. No longer are new people able to join. This pull on the wheel must be corrected if the small group's ministry is to continue, because without growth this is little more than a pastoral group. In this chapter I will look at some of the ways to keep a small group on course, both in terms of adding new members and expanding the number of groups. Because the principles are designed to work in a small group, they can be applied to youth ministries of any size.

Preparing existing members

A small-group ministry won't expand just because a new programme is introduced or even because of the quality of the leaders. Rather, it grows as a result of the young people inviting their friends to join. The mission of small-group leaders is to equip their young people to be dedicated followers of Christ and, through their Christian witness, to lead others to follow their example. With loving support and gentle encouragement, there is almost no limit to what can be achieved by a few.

Envisioning

My daughter calls me 'Daddy'; my parents call me 'Daniel'; and, though I'm not prepared to tell you what my wife calls me, I can reveal that over the years I have been known by many of the youth workers as 'The Metaphor Kid'! This has been due to my frequent use of imagery to communicate vision. Over the years I have used dozens of pictures to communicate not just the text, but hopefully also the heart of what this involves.

In order to launch a new youth ministry for 14-19s, we used many opportunities to share the vision. First, a radio-style advert, offering a quick glimpse of what it was all about and an invitation to find out more, was recorded and distributed to young people in the area who might be interested. Then a local theatre was hired for a presentation at which ideas were swapped and the emerging vision shared. This ended with a clip from the movie, *Field of Dreams*, in which in a cornfield Kevin Costner hears a voice saying, 'If you build it, he will come.' For Costner, this meant constructing a baseball stadium in a sparsely populated rural community in the belief that this would bring back a deceased star player. For the young people, I suggested that it meant getting involved in building a ministry in the belief that Christ would come. After that, an unusual boxing evening was held, which included an inflatable boxing ring, giant boxing gloves and helmets, and a supply of *Rocky* films. This time the young people were challenged literally to 'step into the ring' to indicate their desire to be part of the growing community.

Because new people continue to be added and memories fade, once in a while it will be necessary to remind the whole group of the vision. Ultimately, however, it is up to the small-group leaders to keep it alive. Each young person needs to be constantly made aware that community will only grow when new people are brought into it, and they have a specific contribution to make. This may appear demanding, but I have found that the bigger the challenge the greater the response. Rhetoric alone is never enough; something far more tangible is required. Once I took one of our small or cell groups into the main church hall, and asked them to imagine the day when the youth ministry had grown to such a size it would become necessary to use this as the regular venue. We then talked about which of their friends they could imagine occupying each of the chairs.

One simple way of reminding a group of its potential to grow is to adopt what Willow Creek Community Church have championed as the 'empty chair'. At every gathering, one chair is left vacant as a visible reminder to the group that they need new members. I heard of one small group that purchased an unusual plant pot, in the shape of a mad professor, to be their 'empty chair'. Each week a young person would look after the plant. The 'empty chair' principle may even prompt some groups to pay for one extra cinema ticket or slice of pizza, in the hope that a new person will be available to make use of it each time. The key is regularly and imaginatively to remind the young people of this vision to be a growing community.

Equipping

Most young people enjoy talking to their friends about things like music, football or films, but are intimidated by the 'God' subject. This may be compounded by the pressure leaders may put on them to 'share the faith' and the religious language they are expected to use. Relating what they hear in church with the world their friends inhabit can seem very daunting, so many prefer to live with the 'guilt' of saying nothing. Behind this lies a distorted picture of what evangelism is all about.

I don't want young people to become religious zealots or 'Bible bashers': I simply want them to enjoy being good friends with people and to include in their circle those who don't consider themselves yet to be Christians. If true friendship is about sharing with others the things that matter to us, then young people should be able to talk about their taste in music, the football team they support, the films they have seen and their fantastic youth programme. It should require no more courage to confess to being a West Ham United Football Club supporter than to being a follower of Christ – both rely on miracles! Once group members have grasped this, they can relax and get on with the normal business of sharing with friends the things that are important to them. Naturally enough, these friendships should be real and not exist primarily for evangelistic gain.

To help young people think more about the relationships they have, why not invite them to make a list of their friends and any friendships they might want to develop? They could then consider what time and energy they are prepared to invest in these friendships. The cell-group format often ends with a 'witness' section, when members are regularly encouraged to name and pray for their friends.

Finally, young people who are not Christians can still participate in growing the group. They may not introduce their friends to Christ, but they can still introduce them to his community, the small group. If you see this in general terms, as simply making a 'personal introduction', individuals are then free to respond in the way most appropriate to them.

Encouraging

Though it may be natural, it will also be quite daunting for young people to introduce their friends to the faith, so every attempt they make should be celebrated. This is particularly important when, as will often be the case, their overtures are rejected. An affirming environment will encourage the group to be more adventurous, and those who don't involve their faith in their friendships won't be left feeling as though they are less valuable than those who do.

Adding new members

Contacting

Small or cell groups ministries generally grow because fringe members gradually decide to become more involved. John's Gospel records that, on joining Jesus' small group, the first thing Andrew did was to invite his brother, Simon (who was on the fringe), to get involved too (Jn. 1:40–42). Simon was brought to Jesus and, under the new name of Peter, became a prime 'mover and shaker' in the early church.

No small or cell group meeting will ever satisfy all the needs of all its members, so it is important to establish a rhythm that caters for the varying requirements of those on the fringe as well as the core members. Core members of one small group I know encourage fringe members to participate by inviting them to play football in the local park. After a few games, these fringe members are often more open to joining in other activities, and their journey to faith may begin as a result.

Inviting

Once potential group members have been contacted they need to be invited to further group activities. But what form should these invitations take? There is currently a debate about how best to bring someone who is not a Christian to activities connected with the church. With their roots in the charismatic tradition, many of the cell-church proponents advocate an experiential approach:

potential group members are invited to observe, first-hand, the reality of God in a worship environment. The hope is that though they may not understand all that is happening, they will at least be impressed by the sincerity of the believers and get a sense of God's presence. Others prefer a more rational approach: potential group members are invited to a progression of 'seeker-sensitive' activities that allow them to move forward at their own pace until they have sufficient understanding to choose whether or not to accept Christ.

While I do not deny the validity of the experiential approach, it usually relies on potential members being sufficiently open to spiritual things. In addition, young people are often more confident about bringing their non-Christian friends to seeker-sensitive activities. To be fair, the cell-group model is designed to be inclusive, but those who only read the headings and meeting planners, and who don't have a deeper understanding of cell-church values, often run the risk of over-emphasising the prescribed content of 'welcome, worship, word (and ministry) and witness'.

Each group will need to consider what activities may be appropriate for potential members. What may begin as an informal game of football in a local park should, in time, progress to something more demanding. This may mean providing a Youth Alpha or 'just looking' course, but this should never happen at the expense of a healthy social calendar. Remember, it is during informal activities that potential members frequently judge whether or not the group offers authentic community.

Challenging

For some, becoming a Christian happens in a moment. For others, it is a gradual journey towards faith in Christ.

But everyone has to go through the stage when they must decide whether or not they want to be a dedicated follower of Christ. Those who opt in may find their values begin to change – perhaps dramatically, perhaps quite slowly – as they appreciate the privilege and the challenge of living a Christ-centred life. It is vital at this crucial time that leaders don't impose cultural or ethical values. For example, some may believe smoking to be anti-social behaviour or even incompatible with the Christian faith, but this will be a secondary issue for most new believers. It is more important that they are established within the growing community, with people around them who can provide appropriate support and encouragement at a significant time in their lives.

Equipping

Those new to a group, and particularly to the Christian faith, are often better at inviting others to join than those who have been in the group longer. Yet, all too often, many new believers become so absorbed in the community that they neglect those they used to spend time with. Where this happens small or cell groups rarely grow, so it is vital that new members maintain long-standing friendships with people outside. They will also need opportunities to introduce these friends to the group, and it is advisable to agree on a few activities to facilitate this. The new member might invite his friends to an activity, or arrange for group members to go to something organised by his friends. Either way, it could lead to further expansion of the fringe membership.

Richard appeared quiet and lacking in confidence when he first joined the group, but developed a habit of frequently bringing guests to group activities. At first this came as a surprise, but eventually the other group members began to take notice of what he was doing. He clearly challenged them, and they too began to think of people they could invite. The fact that Richard was so quiet only served to inspire them all the more.

Multiplying new groups

An intentional small-group ministry is different from a small youth group in that its growth always leads to the formation of more small or cell groups rather than the enlargement of the one 'whole group'. Small or cell groups seeking to be growing communities should not be surprised when more young people join them, and they should ensure that plans to form new groups are in place long before existing ones become too big. Many groups lose the initiative by giving this important issue too little attention too late. When the need becomes urgent, not enough care is taken to multiply the groups in positive and healthy ways and, as a result, some never survive the process. Just as the birth of a new child involves a number of stages, so too does the formation of a new group.

Conception

The birth of a 'daughter' group begins with the decision to create it and, as in all happy partnerships, this must be a joint decision by the small-group leader and the group members themselves. They must also agree on the timing. When will the 'mother' group be ready to release the new 'daughter' group? When will the 'daughter' be ready to leave? Preparation to create a 'daughter' should begin not when the 'mother' group is approaching capacity but when membership is still at its lowest.

Youth ministries with only five young people have the basic ingredients of an intentional small or cell group ministry. Starting with just one small or cell group enables the ministry to give greater attention to create the right values and ethos. The first group takes on extra significance as it becomes the source of all those that follow. Because each successive generation carries with it some of the characteristics of its forebears, it is possible for smaller youth ministries to give their first group the right start in life. Larger youth ministries can create the same conditions by choosing to restrict themselves to launching just one pilot group – instead of a multitude. This prototype group can then be used to develop a core of young people who subsequently become leaders in the next generation of small or cell groups.

Pregnancy

Starting with the very first meeting of the 'mother' group, the intention to create other groups should be clearly articulated and regularly repeated. However, acknowledging the intention is not enough; the young people must understand the implications and accept, as a spiritual challenge, the need to create a new small group and to work towards that end. Give positive reasons why forming a new group is in everyone's best interest. Then, as membership increases, anticipation rises, and the resulting new group is seen as a success rather than a disappointment. Throughout this process it is important to keep the vision alive, and visible reminders, such as the 'empty chair' described earlier, will prove very effective.

As the delivery date approaches, it is quite normal for those in the 'mother' group to express concerns about some of the changes required as a result of the new arrival. These concerns need to be listened to and fully talked through before any solutions are decided on. Often questions arise as to which of the existing members will go to form the new group, and what effect this will have on established relationships. The 'no rules' principle, allowing people freedom to do whatever works for them (within limited boundaries), is particularly important at this point. Group members are often reassured by the knowledge that they can still be in the group of their choice. Because the addition of new members multiplies the total number of possible friendships, very often a growing small group will naturally form two or more cliques, which in turn become the nucleus of the new group(s). The 'no rules' principle ensures that close friends can remain in the same group, leaving others from the wider circle of friends to form a group of their own.

It is helpful to practice various aspects of the delivery in advance of the birth, as this prepares the young people for the inevitable change. One simple idea is to begin making use of sub-groups for specific tasks some time before the delivery date. Some sessions might begin and end with everyone together, but the two sub-groups could meet separately during the main part of the programme. Nearer the delivery date, the two sub-groups might occasionally meet on their own for the whole session, even at a different venue. This gives the small-group leader an opportunity to observe the likely membership size and dynamics of both groups, and helps members to familiarise themselves with the new arrangements.

As well as preparing the young people, it is also necessary to have ready a new small-group leader and assistant. The smoothest transition usually occurs when the assistant in the 'mother' group becomes leader of the 'daughter' group. This person will already have a good relationship with the core members and so be able to satisfy their need for stability. Small or cell groups that intend to set up new groups need to ensure they have a good assistant already in place. With just a couple of weeks before the delivery date, it is too late to bring an unknown individual into the group and expect instant community. In addition, as soon as the new small group has been formed both leaders will require new assistants, so they will have to start identifying possible candidates at an early stage.

Delivery

It may have taken many months to arrive, but eventually the pregnancy will come to a dramatic conclusion with the birth of the new 'daughter'. Inevitably, there will be a mixture of anxiety and joy as the new group is released into the world. This is a time to celebrate, and many small-group ministries host special parties to mark the great occasion. This, after all, is what the young people and their leaders have been waiting for.

Both the 'daughter' and 'mother' groups need carefully planned opportunities to celebrate the birth; the former to create expectation and the latter to overcome loss. The first session is, in effect, the start of a new life for both groups, and this should be seen as positive and challenging. Often the birth creates extra opportunity for introducing potential members to both groups, so appropriate activities should be planned to encourage this. There can be no better way to launch a small group than to introduce new people into it, particularly if they are not yet Christians.

Post-delivery

Both 'daughter' and 'mother' groups will need to evolve fresh patterns of operating. This will include the development of new contracts and the gradual acceptance of the new roles played by members. To ensure the continued growth of the ministry, it is important that both groups begin to establish plans for the next generation of 'daughters'. Both leaders should immediately begin to prepare their members for growth and subsequent multiplication by making full use of visual reminders such as the 'empty chair' and resuming the search for future leaders. Incidentally, small or cell groups are 'multiplied', not 'added', because each successive generation leads to the establishment of more groups. Starting from one, the multiplication effect should be one, two, four, eight, sixteen, and so on.

One month after 'delivery', it may be helpful to organise a reunion in which both groups come together for a shared activity. This is a time to appreciate the success of each and to reassure anxious members that the changes are working. From then on, an informal link can be maintained, but with each successive multiplication the need to reunite old groups becomes significantly less. In any case, the regular 'big group' activities, when they all come together, will provide sufficient opportunity for interaction.

Each group should aim to form a new one, on average, every twelve to eighteen months. This requires careful thought and advance planning – something youth workers are not always renowned for! It is important to create time to discuss with small-group leaders where they see the opportunities for group multiplication and who is showing potential as a small-group leader. What excites me most is that many of the young people who will join these small or cell groups aren't even aware of the youth ministry's existence yet. In time, they will be drawn in by the young people who already come, and invited to join the fringe. A number will go on to become dedicated followers of Christ and help launch new groups, once again multiplying the growing community.

Homework

- List five ways in which you will motivate your young people to introduce friends either to the small group or to the Christian faith.

....

....

....

....

....

- List five activities that will help your small group to expand its fringe membership.

....

....

....

....

....

- How many core members does a small group need to have before you believe it is too full? When will your group reach this point?

....

....

....

- When your group creates a new one, who will be the new leader and assistant?

....

....

....

11

Small groups, big communication

On leaving school, I worked for the exclusive bank, Messrs Coutts & Co. On my first day I was assigned to the City of London branch to work in stock and share settlements. My job was to help settle the trading accounts of bank customers who had bought and sold shares or bonds. On the fortnightly Settlement Days my world went nuts. I would frantically add up, subtract, multiply, in fact do almost anything to get the books to balance. It soon became clear I was not suited to this work. I had never been good at maths and was not what could be described as a 'detail' person. On one occasion I credited the wrong account with an obscene amount of money which should have been allocated to a corporate account. This was only made worse by the fact that it was over a bank holiday weekend, thus costing the bank even more to correct.

My difficulties at the bank were compounded by the learning methods employed at the time. I was told to complete a pink form for every white one, that every credit had to have a debit and what codes to use in the antiquated computer system. But no one ever told me why I had to do this, or what would happen if I didn't follow all the lists and rules. I wanted to know what happened to all the pink and white forms and where all the money came from and went to, but this was thought unnecessary. As a result I made silly mistakes.

Communication is both an art and a science, and different people require different approaches. There are those, like me, who need to see the 'big picture', and there are those who are fascinated and reassured by 'detail'. In this chapter I will introduce some of the skills and ideas I have found helpful in a small group context.

Learning principles

I have deliberately resisted raising until now the subject of communication – what it is youth ministries want to convey to the young people, and how to go about it – in order to give sufficient emphasis to the relational purpose of small or cell groups. A community has to be joined, not just attended. While some types of small group, such as the Youth Alpha course, rely on their programme content for their raison d'être, most don't need to. The example set for the young people by the leader, and by the values they adopt, is far more significant than the chosen message or programme. This said, let me introduce three communication principles which I believe to be important.

Purpose

Jesus' 'great commission' was to make disciples – to bring people to that defining moment in their faith-journey and to show them how to obey his teaching (Mt. 28:19, 20). The emphasis is firmly on application as opposed to knowledge. Bible study should always lead to personal transformation: anything short of this is missing the point. Fixed in the small-group leader's mind must always be the question 'So what?' When a passage from the Bible is read, the young people should be encouraged to consider how it relates to their lives and what it demands of them.

Informal education

Some youth ministries design their small or cell groups to be no more than an intimate means of religious instruction. Group members are allowed to ask questions, but these only ever relate to the topic selected by the leader. In practice, it is the leader who asks most of the questions, otherwise they won't know if the religious instruction has been absorbed. This type of small group is programme-driven, with each meeting used to deliver the next prescribed session plan. When this does not work, a new and more dynamic programme is sought. Many churches use adult house groups in this way, seeing them as an extension of Sunday sermons, either to supplement the Christian education programme or, worse still, as a kind of comprehension test for slow learners. The danger is that some groups may fall short of their potential because older leaders repeat this learning style with their young group members.

Because a small group is a community that young people belong to, and not a club they attend, there is great scope here for informal education. The role of the leader changes from being instructor to facilitator, and it is the questions asked by the young people that determine the agenda, not *vice versa*. I have written more extensively about this in *Joined Up: An Introduction to Youth Work and Ministry*. Using an informal education approach, an argument between two members might

prompt a discussion on conflict resolution; mentioning a
television soap could lead to questions about sexuality;
someone's negative situation might generate an explo-
ration of Christ's view of life. In all these examples, it is
highly unlikely that a programme would coincide with
the precise timing or detail of the young people's questions. Their learning is enhanced by the flexible response
of the informal educator. This can appear daunting at
first, but leaders should never underestimate the positive effect they have on their group members. Simply
spending time together discussing a range of issues and
seeking biblical answers to current problems, is 90 per
cent of the ministry.

One small group I worked with comprised fifteen-
year-old lads. On one occasion, one of them said, 'I can
believe Jesus was the Son of God, that he performed
miracles and that he will come back again. But what I
can't believe is that anyone – not even Christ – could be
so nice all of the time.' This statement troubled me
because I felt it showed an incomplete understanding of
Jesus. I made a mental note to return to this before the
end of the session, by which time I had found an excuse
to position an old table in the centre of the room.
Referring back to the earlier statement, I read aloud, in
a casual voice, the account of Jesus turning over the
tables in the temple (Mk. 11:15–17). I then read it again,
only this time injecting as much passion and drama as I
could muster. The reading culminated in me kicking
and smashing the old table to bits. The young people
were stunned! Once the adrenaline had stopped racing,
I asked them if they still thought Jesus was always so
'nice'. I challenged them to read the Gospels and
observe how Jesus treated people.

On another occasion with the same group, someone
asked why the Gospel writers were inconsistent in their

details of Jesus' life and work. On hearing this, I stood up, stretched out my arms and ran round the room with my jumper over my head, shouting, 'I'm a little teapot, short and stout.' I concluded with a forward roll on the carpet. Once again, the group was stunned. I gave each of them a piece of paper, a pen and two minutes in which to record what they had just observed. A few concentrated on the chronological detail, while others focused more on the emotions. All were right in what they said, but none of them had the complete picture. Yet, taken together, they would have enabled those who had not seen the incident to understand what had happened. We used this experiment to think why the four Gospel writers might have recorded different detail, but we also recognised the many similarities between the accounts.

I tell you these incidents to highlight what can be achieved by responding directly to young people's questions rather than simply pursuing the prescribed programme. This approach does require the leader to be flexible enough to respond in a meaningful way and I recognise this may be somewhat challenging, particularly for those with less experience to draw on. However, the leader's response does not always have to be instantaneous. It is better to react a week later, having had time to consider the best method, than to respond immediately and badly or do nothing at all.

Informal education does not assume that the role of the educator is always to be right. I have to accept that there are many questions relating to faith and life which I do not have an answer for. When I am asked these questions, all I can say is 'I don't know. You tell me.' Even when I think I do have an answer, it is not always appropriate for me to deliver it as a 'fact'. Instead, I say, 'This is what I believe. What do you think?' The leader should always seek to help the young people decide what they personally believe, not follow the evangelical tradition of telling them what they should believe.[18] After all, the aim is to create a community, not a cult. I believe this approach conveys respect for the individual and confidence in the validity of the Gospel.

Creativity

Somebody once told me that I was too creative and not spiritually powerful enough, the inference being that creativity and spirituality are mutually exclusive. However, this dualistic attitude does not match what we find in the Bible. The Genesis account of creation is rich in imagery and awesome spiritual power, and many Old Testament heroes were creative in their prophetic ministries.[19] And surely no one could ever accuse Jesus of rejecting spiritual power in favour of creativity? In the New Testament, the Gospel writers are keen to highlight his creative approach to his ministry.[20] Even the Word had to become flesh in order for human beings to grasp God's nature (Jn. 1:1–14). We are made in the image of a creative and powerful God, and this should lead us to experiment with our God-given qualities.

Small-group leaders need to employ every resource available to them as they seek to communicate with their young people. Teaching alone is not sufficient: the task of the leader is to bring to life what otherwise would remain theoretical in the minds of the group. Later, I will introduce some creative communication methods, but in the meantime I simply plead for leaders to be bold in using their creativity, to see themselves as spiritual versions of Walt Disney's 'Imagineers'.[21]

Learning styles

All youth ministries have at least one person who talks when he is meant to be listening, who is apathetic when everyone else is enthusiastic, whose body language is off-putting. But it may be that he is simply bored or de-motivated by the leader's style of communication. Leaders may be tempted to label this person as 'difficult' rather than admit their own inability to communicate. However, educationalists believe that it is possible to tailor communication according to an individual's approach to learning. There are three basic learning styles, and a brief understanding of these may help leaders become more responsive to the needs of their groups.[22]

Symbolic learners

Strange as it may sound, some people listen more with their eyes than their ears. For them, a moving image, a picture or an object can communicate in a way that words alone cannot. They are feelings-oriented, needing to experience something before they can understand it. Those with this symbolic learning style are stimulated by the human senses of sight, sound, taste, touch and smell. Jesus used this approach when he initiated what has become known as the Lord's Supper, which communicates forgiveness through all five senses. Vivid story-telling, drama, poetry and parables are all helpful to symbolic learners, who also gain much from sharing each other's experiences. For them, the key question is 'Why do I need to know this?'

Analytic learners

Some people are motivated by facts, lists, 'how tos', and matters of detail. They enjoy the intellectual challenge of testing the validity of information and theories. They find the sensory approach 'fluffy'. Those with an analytical learning style like to listen to what the experts have to say, and are quite content to search for answers to their own questions. They need all the facts before they can make a decision. Jesus used this approach in much of his 'sermon on the mount' (Mt. 5–7). For analytical learners, the key question is 'What do I need to know?'

Pragmatic learners

Some people have a dominant sixth sense – common sense. They are bored by what they perceive to be fruitless discussions, and are sceptical of 'touchy-feely' meetings. For them, the real action is somewhere else. They have lots of ideas and some of these may even be practical. Jesus used this approach when he commissioned his disciples (Mt. 10:1–16; Lk. 10:1–12) to be 'doers of the word'. Pragmatic learners don't need all the facts before they go because they are quite content to solve any problems as they encounter them. In fact, their understanding is reliant on being able to see how everything works in practice. For them, the key question is 'How does this work?'

Recognising these learning styles may help you tailor the content of your group sessions to the specific needs of individuals. A small or cell group comprising mainly pragmatic learners will be most successful when it focuses on putting faith into action. For them, meeting angels or searching for Christ is best understood by serving the needs of the poor, then reflecting on what they have discovered (Heb. 13:2; Mt. 25:44, 45). However, a group of symbolic learners are helped when those who have 'found Christ' share their experiences and the group works together to produce an appropriate symbol. The analytic learners, on the other hand, will want to know the facts. When did so-and-so 'find Christ'? What were the circumstances? And so on. All learning styles are of equal value, but, historically, evangelical Christianity has tended to concentrate on the analytic. This might be why some people fail to make a connection with faith.

Learning tools

Recognising how each individual learns is half the battle; knowing what to do next is the other half. On the basis that a youth worker is only as good as the last idea they begged, borrowed or stole, let me provide you with a few possibilities. This list is by no means exhaustive, and those of you who are more creative than I will no doubt already have 'been there, done that, written the book'.

Location

Much of Jesus' teaching took place in the open air, where everyday surroundings could be used to great effect. Watching daily rural life probably led to the parable of the sower (Lk. 8:1–15); regular boat trips across the Sea of Galilee provided the background to many discussions on faith (Mt. 14:22–34). With a little imagination, it is possible to create the same effect by 'imagineering' the right conditions. Informal educators seek to create what John Dewey called 'forked-road' situations which present individuals with dilemmas and choices[23].

A leader might take his group out into a cornfield and ask them what biblical parallels they can find. Some may see a parallel with the parable of the sower, while others may recognise the need for harvesters to gather in the crop (Mt. 9:37, 38). A country path that leads to a 'fork' could prompt discussion on guidance and choices. The possibilities are endless. The small size of the group makes it ideally suited to such informal activities. Meeting times can be changed, transport and supervision (if required) easily arranged. The change of location is often sufficient to break the routine and force each member to think more deeply.

Storytelling

Jesus was the master storyteller. Using simple language and examples from everyday life, he painted vivid pictures in people's minds to help them understand his message. Storytelling is currently experiencing a revival in popular culture, as comedians take on pop star status and fill venues with their stand-up routines and commentary on 'life'. The small or cell group context is particularly conducive to the use of stories and illustrations because of the high emphasis on communal learning.

Focus

For the benefit of symbolic learners, it may be helpful to include an obvious focus that allows the young people to respond in a meaningful way. The more historic churches have a distinct advantage at this point, for they already appreciate the value of imagery and visual statements. A good focal point allows sufficient scope for people's minds to wander, but not so much that they never come back.

A simple idea could be to light a candle and ask someone to read John 8:12, where Jesus describes himself as 'the light of the world'. Then invite the rest of the group to light their own candles from the one source of light, as a sign of their commitment to let their light shine before their friends (Mt. 5:14–16). At a recent worship night, the theme was experiencing God's refreshment (Jn. 4:7–26). A large container of iced water was placed in the middle of the room. In their own time, the group members were invited to come and experience refreshment, either drinking or washing their hands in the cold water (one or other, not both!). The physical response of standing up and then experiencing the cold water became a powerful prayer of acceptance.

Video

Because we live in a visual-dominated age, small-group leaders should make the use of appropriate video material a regular part of group life. Though this may include some specifically Christian programmes, a general release film or made-for-TV programme can be just as effective. Watching a film together helps to grow community and establishes a point of contact between faith and reality. If Paul could use material from popular culture to communicate his message (Acts 17:28), then I feel quite confident that I can too. Hollywood movie-makers are very proficient at capturing the mood of popular culture, and often reference to a particular clip prompts energetic discussion. However, I should like to add a word of caution at this point. Video is not the sole answer to contemporary communication and should therefore be used sparingly.

Domestic video cameras are now widely available and capable of producing material to a high standard. With a little imagination, they can be used to great effect. Once, to introduce the topic of 'What are you like when no one is watching', a co-worker and I secretly filmed inside the bedrooms of two of our group members (we knew they would appreciate the attention!). Showing the results was great fun and a helpful starting point for the theme. However, the best use of a video camera is to place it in the hands of the young people themselves; send them out to interpret an agreed topic on film. Not only will they have great fun, they will also be concentrating on the issue and analysing the effectiveness of what they are creating. Watching the final product and discussing the choice of edits can prove very constructive.

Finally ...

A small or cell groups ministry that seeks to avoid being programme-driven must rely on the creative resources within the group. You can train yourself to become more creative: pooling people's creative ideas; observing what others do and how they achieve it, and building on the ideas of other groups. Start with a topic and then think randomly, connecting your thoughts with opposites, parallels, similes and word associations. Write and draw on paper as you go, until you have the beginnings of a workable idea.

Homework

- Think of someone in your group who finds it difficult to concentrate during a session, or is 'disruptive'. Reflect on how he/she signals dissatisfaction and how you respond to this. Acknowledging his/her learning style, what strategy will you adopt in the future?

Young person's name:

....

His/her negative signals:

....

....

....

Your current response:

....

....

....

His/her learning style:

....

Your future response:

....

....

....

- List five different locations you could informally use to develop your small group.

Location	Purpose

12

Small groups, big challenge

'Let's go deep sea fishing,' he said.
'The sea won't be rough,' he said.
'You'll love it,' he said.

I had to admit, as the boat left the idyllic West Country fishing port, that it did indeed seem like a good idea. Ahead lay six hours of fishing, eating, chatting and ... waves.

'Waves? You didn't say anything about waves,' I protested. As the boat made its way out into the English Channel, I clung to the railings and told myself everything was fine. I lied. Twenty minutes after we left *terra firma*, I began to feel sick.

'Hang loose,' I told myself. 'Better to get "it" out of your system.' So I did. Fortunately, I managed to position myself downwind and over the side of the boat. A fellow passenger made a joke about my generosity in providing the ground-bait. But I wasn't laughing.

When land was but a distant dream, the boat stopped and we began to fish. Threading the line through the eyeholes was nauseating. So too was the fishing. Come to think of it, even breathing seemed to make matters worse. I could hardly focus on the end of the rod. The boat was now completely at the mercy of the waves ...

'So, tell me ... er ... what happens if we – well, you know – sink?' I asked, but no one was listening. They were all too busy enjoying themselves. I caught a few fish but couldn't bring myself to reel them in. My problem wasn't so much ethical as physical. By this point I was throwing up every fifteen minutes. There were still five hours of fishing left and absolutely no means of escape. I decided the best strategy was a defensive one. I put down my fishing rod and sat staring into the distance. By fixing my gaze at the horizon, I found that the sickness subsided. The moment I looked elsewhere, I was sick again. For the next few hours I was truly focused, to the point that my neck began to hurt. But it worked. The boat eventually docked, and I leapt off and kissed the ground. (I wonder if the Pope gets travel-sick, too.)

Be focused

I learnt two things from that fateful day. First, never believe a friendly sea dog (even if he is a close friend, fellow youth worker and small-group member). Second, always remain focused, particularly when the going is rough. In this chapter, I want to draw the threads together so that you are able to develop your own response to all you have read. If, as a result, you want to make any changes, either introducing a new small-group ministry or adjusting an established one, then you will need to focus on the task ahead. Be clear about what you are seeking to do. When do you want to achieve it, and whose support do you require?

On one occasion, Simon Peter found himself in a similarly challenging situation – on a boat some distance from the shore and buffeted by the waves (Mt. 14:22–34; Jn. 6:16–21). The wind was strong, the waves high and the disciples were finding the going tough. To their astonishment, they looked up to see Jesus walking towards them across the water. One of them shouted, 'It's a ghost!'

Peter, being an experienced fisherman, probably had a 'sea dog' reputation to maintain, so he said, 'If it's really you, Lord, tell me to come to you on the water.' And Jesus simply replied, 'Come.' Peter found himself faced with a life-changing challenge, a 'forked-road' situation. Should he accept the challenge and risk his future? Should he opt for the easy life and risk regretting what might have been? Slowly, he stood up, released his grip of the boat, finger by finger, and set out to walk on the water. As long as he remained 'focused' on Christ, he was secure.

Could it be for you that what began as a general interest in small or cell groups has become a life-changing challenge to do something significant? Once again Jesus is saying, 'Come.' You too face a 'forked-road' situation. Do you accept the challenge of growing community and risk the unknown? Do you opt for the easy life and risk regretting what might have been? My hope is that, finger by finger, you will release your grip and commit yourself to developing an intentional small or cell group ministry.

Be willing

Peter had become a dedicated follower of Christ when Jesus noticed him and his brother, Andrew, fishing (Mt. 4:18–20). 'Come, follow me,' he had called to them, 'and I will make you fishers of men.' From that moment,

Peter left his nets and didn't look back. Only later was he to discover what his bold move would involve. For the present, it was sufficient to know that he was willing to leave security behind and join others in accompanying Jesus in an uncertain and sometimes dangerous enterprise. But, though Peter may not have understood it at the time, Jesus always intended that those who followed him should help others join his growing community.

Take a moment to think back to the time when you first encountered Jesus. In becoming part of his community, you are also called to 'fish' for potential fellow disciples. Ask yourself, 'To what extent is this a current reality for me?' The young people in your neighbourhood are your potential catch – but, being truthful, how much real fishing is being done? More to the point, how many fish are actually being caught? These are challenging questions that all Christians have to answer.

Be ready

After Jesus' death and resurrection, Peter and the other disciples temporarily returned to what had once been familiar – fishing (Jn. 21:1–14). During their time away they had apparently lost the knack, so that night they caught nothing. When Jesus shouted from the shore that they should throw their net to the right side of the boat, they obeyed – and caught so many fish it was a struggle to haul in the net. In all, there were 153 large ones.

This is the kind of catch all fishermen dream of but rarely achieve. On the local canal, people fish for hours, sometimes even through the night, yet I have never met anyone who has caught more than a dozen fish. Their single-line fishing rods are simply not capable of catching large numbers. Could it be that in fishing for young people, many youth ministries are using rods held by 'experts' when they could have been using nets? Let me explain.

An intentional small-group ministry is similar to a net – it has a wide coverage and can catch all types. Picture in your mind a large net with its interlocking vertical and horizontal cords. The horizontal lines represent the small-group leaders, the vertical ones the group members. At every point where the lines cross, a knot is created – this symbolises a relationship between the two. Using this analogy, an intentional small or cell groups ministry creates a network of relationships which, when used at Christ's direction, can be used to draw in many young people. The bigger the net, the greater the catch. There will always be a need for high-profile events and creative programmes, but these will never replace the basic human need for community and identity.

Let the adventure begin.

Homework

- What do you believe are the key changes that need to take place in your youth/small or cell group ministry?

....

....

....

....

....

• What are your priorities?

This month: ....

....

....

This term: ....

....

....

This year:..

....

....

• Which of the key decision-makers in your youth ministry or church do you need to spend time with if your small group ideas are to be considered?

....

....

....

- Who else needs to read this book, and how many copies should you order?

....

....

....

Part 3

RESOURCING GROUPS

13

Small groups, big fellowship ideas

Sports

Sport can be a great asset to a small-group ministry in uniting people together under a common cause. A group that works well together as a team is likely to be successful in other areas.

1. Few-a-side football/netball

The small size of each group should enable few-a-side football/netball teams to be formed. If your small or cell groups ministry comprises a number of groups, organise a competition or league table. To be fully inclusive, ask each team to play two rounds – one of football, the other of netball. You may be able to borrow a local sports facility. Alternatively, why not hire part of a sports hall at your local leisure centre?

2. Small group Olympics

Host an alternative Olympics in which each event requires minimum activity. These might include little-finger wrestling, ten-metre walkathon, throwing the matchstick, synchronised sitting, and so on. This surreal event will work best if all participants are encouraged to come dressed in sports attire. Provide small awards for the least amount of effort invested. An alternative is to ask people to each bring a sleeping bag, and to host the Sleeping Bag Olympics, with each event requiring participants to compete in their sleeping bags. Examples could include high-jumping, sprinting, gymnastics and volleyball.

3. Cheer leaders

Arrange to watch a local match – this might be an amateur/semi-professional football/netball team, or one belonging to a school. If a group member is playing, it is always encouraging if the rest of the group turns up to watch and cheer them on from the sidelines.

4. Leisure centres

Local leisure centres are usually able to provide a wide range of sports and activities which small or cell groups can make good use of. These might include swimming, scuba-diving, table tennis, badminton, squash, basketball, netball, trampolining and even, in some cases, rock-climbing. Find out from your local leisure centre what sports are on offer.

5. Water or snowball fight

Summer and winter can bring opportunities for impromptu water or snowball fights. These may be difficult to schedule, so you will need to rely on the group's flexibility. If the weather conditions suddenly prove conducive, invite them round for a fight. Text them the meeting point. Better still, ambush them!

6. Fitness programme

Many young people are concerned about improving physical strength or reducing weight. Either way, why not join them? Don't offer advice unless you are qualified; instead, enrol on an appropriate fitness programme together. Alternatively, you could all arrange to go jogging or cycling.

Food

Friends having a meal is an excellent way of socialising, particularly after a sporting event. Here are some culinary ideas to get you started.

7. DIY pizza party

Ask everyone to bring a pizza base plus one topping of their choice. Have fun creating and cooking imaginative pizzas. Be prepared to spend hours cleaning the oven and re-painting the ceiling afterwards!

8. Pudding party

Each person brings a pudding, and you all spend the evening consuming obscene quantities of sweet dishes.

9. A moving feast

Invite your group members to a slap-up meal, with each course served at a different location. Possible hosts could include the young people themselves, their parents or other church members. Some ideas to add variety include:

- Providing a different national dish at each location.

- Travelling between locations using the most unusual form of wheeled transport.

- Serving the courses in reverse order, starting with coffee and mints.

- Revealing the precise location of each venue clue by clue.

- Making the event a World Vision 24-hour Famine Moving Fast.

Remember to thank your hosts afterwards, and offer to pay any expenses.

10. Master chef

Invite the group to cook themselves a gourmet meal in your kitchen. They will need to agree on the menu, provide their own ingredients, divide up the tasks and ensure that the washing-up is done afterwards. Thought should also be given to table decoration and dress code. As well as being a lot of fun, this presents an opportunity to observe teamwork and the young people's attitude to domestic chores.

Food market

This is most effective when small or cell groups compete against each other, though it can also work if the young people from one group work in pairs. Provide enough food, cooking utensils, cutlery and crockery for everyone, but divide the assorted items unevenly among the groups. The object of the exercise is for each person to eat the right meal using only the right ingredients and equipment. They do this by bartering with others to obtain what they need. Some may start with all the bread but no butter, while others may have all the knives but no plates. Set a time and space limit for the groups to eat their meal.

Ready, Steady, Cook

Based on the successful television programme, one or two young members purchase the ingredients up to the maximum value of £5. The rest of the group must then turn the assorted items into a culinary delight. The young chefs should have twenty minutes to transform their ingredients into something edible. Expect chaos in the kitchen and a lot of fun in the process.

Residentials

There is something quite special about the time spent together away from the usual routine. Providing a residential experience need not be a complicated affair. Here are some ideas to get you going.

13. Sleep-overs

This simple idea involves all the group members spending the night at someone's house. The event could include food, films and a lot of chat. Be careful to establish the right impression with parents. It may be more appropriate to use the house of a group member than your own, especially if you live alone.

14. Festivals

Each year there are a number of festivals organised for young people, many of which are established as Christian events. These include Spring Harvest, Cross Rhythms, Greenbelt and Soul Survivor. Because the programmes are provided by the festival organisers, it can be comparatively easy to take a small group to these events. All you need do is provide transportation and, in some cases, camping facilities. Group members will usually find being with thousands of other like-minded young people very encouraging.

15. Camping

Camping can be a fun and cheap way of spending some days away. With a few telephone inquiries, it is usually possible to borrow enough of the right equipment and secure a cheap campsite. Be careful not to take young people into hazardous conditions unless you have an appropriate outdoor qualification such as the Summer Mountain Leaders Certificate.

The Youth Hostel Association (YHA) have launched a 'Camping Barns' scheme to provide low-cost camping facilities under a roof. Camping barns are often no more than old farm buildings, but they are cheap, sheltered and have access to cold water and toilet facilities. Further details can be obtained from the YHA.

Service projects

Being able to focus on the needs of others is a healthy way of drawing a group together. Here are some ideas to get you serving.

16. Carol singing

Christmas is an ideal opportunity to do something positive. Your group could go carol singing, visiting local people who are housebound or in residential care homes. Don't do this for money but as a means of bringing Christmas joy to those who are isolated. Arrange to meet at someone's house afterwards for hot mince pies and coffee. Of course, this need not happen only in December. Try it in July!

17. Visiting

Most local communities have a residential care home of some sort or other. As a group, make a regular commitment to visit the residents and spend time with them. You will need to negotiate this with the centre staff, and stress to your group the importance of long-term commitment. What may begin as a noble duty may soon become a joy and privilege.

18. Celebrations

Ask your group to throw a surprise party for someone. Consider who to invite, how to decorate the venue and what to provide. The aim should not be to embarrass someone, but rather to recognise their contribution to community life.

19. Collections

There are always charitable organisations in need of donated items. At Christmas, the group could donate brand new toys to be distributed to children by your local social services office. Alternatively, contact a homeless project and find out what items their clients require. These may vary from new toothbrushes to underpants.

20. Sponsored events

There are a number of charitable organisations that encourage people to raise funds for them in novel ways. World Vision's 24-hour Famine has become an institution among many young people and is well worth getting involved in. The group enjoys a fast-moving programme while not eating for twenty-four hours. Make sure all sponsor money is properly accounted for. Be sensitive to issues relating to weight, diet and food.

14

Small groups, big discipleship ideas

21. *Leap of Faith*

Show the clip from the movie *Leap of Faith* that depicts Steve Martin manipulating his audience. Ask the young people how they can be sure you are not doing to them a more subtle version of the same? Don't accept simplistic statements or polite compliments and, if necessary, be provocative. By the end of the discussion the group should have determined by what criteria they judge both you and the youth ministry. At a later date, you might like to consider creating a (safe) test to ensure they have remembered their criteria.

22. *Last Supper*

Arrange to meet your group at McDonalds (or equivalent) and place an order. Use the opportunity to find out things like how their week has been, what their burger-eating record is, what menu item is most like their character. Then again, you could simply discuss sport. Towards the end of your time together, take some of the remaining drink and a leftover burger (or fries) and use these to remind the group of the last meal the disciples had with Jesus. Read either Luke 22:14–20 or I Corinthians 11:23–26, and recall that Jesus used a relaxed meal and whatever was left over to discuss his death. And there wasn't a lace cloth or tray of glass thimbles in sight. At a suitable moment, invite the young people to take a sip of drink and a piece of burger (or fries) each, and to remember Christ's sacrifice.

23. *Empty vessels*

You will need a washing-up bowl, a transparent jug or container, a large quantity of junk items or rubble, and a supply of water. With your group sitting around you, explain that each of you is meant to be full of God. As you say this, fill the transparent container with water. Explain that we all tend to have junk or rubble items in our lives that limit our God-capacity. Ask each person to select a piece of junk or rubble and relate it to a destructive element in their lives. Invite them to state what the item represents and then place them in the transparent container. This should result in water being displaced à la Archimedes and all that!

Having so much junk in our lives reduces our capacity for God. Correspondingly, if we want more of God we need to ask him to remove more of this junk. Take out the junk items, observing how much water has been displaced, then pour more and more water into the container. Use this as an opportunity to pray for each other to be filled with the Holy Spirit.

24. *New Year hopes and dreams*

At the beginning of the new year, ask your group to dream some dreams. Give them a piece of paper each and ask them to write down what they hope to achieve during the next six months, where they want to be in relation to God and what they hope will have happened in the group. Then give each person an envelope. Ask the group to write their names and full addresses on their envelopes and seal their papers inside. Explain that you will keep the sealed envelopes safe and post them back in six months' time.

25. Wayne's World

Show the clip from the movie *Wayne's World* which depicts the two lads parking their car on the edge of an airport runway, lying on their car roof and watching the planes take off and land.[24] As they do this, they discuss 'life'. If you are close to one and mad enough, why not take your group to the outer perimeter of an airport and do the same?

26. Star-gazing

Arrange for your group to meet in the open and when it is dark. All lie on your backs and gaze up at the stars, and consider how big the cosmos is and how big God is. Recently, on a residential camp, I discovered a lot about stars from the young people I was with. Did you know that some stars are so far away, by the time we receive their light they may have ceased to exist? Spooky, eh! Read some appropriate Bible verses such as Matthew 6:25–34.

27. Cool bucket

Provide a large container of ice-chilled water and a ladle. Ask the group to recall an incident when they were particularly thirsty. Initiate a discussion on God's ability to refresh people. Read John 4:13, 14 and invite those who want to be refreshed by God's 'living water' to take some of the ice-chilled water. They might want to drink it, give a cup to someone in the group, or wash their hands, face or feet. Their actions will be symbolic of their desire for God to refresh them.

28. Woolly prayers

Obtain a large ball of wool and arrange the group in a circle. Tie one end of the wool around your ankle or wrist and lead the group in a short prayer. Then throw the ball of wool to another member of the group, calling them by name. On catching the ball, this person must wrap the wool around one part of their body and lead the group in another short prayer. Once completed, they repeat the process by throwing the ball of wool to another group member. Continue until you have run out of wool and the group is completely intertwined with wool. Alternatively, use the same activity to initiate conversation about what it means to be members of the body of Christ.

29. Pray in the dark

Obtain a supply of fluorescent paint and reflective strips, together with large sheets of black paper or card. Invite the group to display key words on the card using the paint and florescent strips. The words could relate to a Bible passage that you have been studying. Once completed, display the cards on the walls of the room. Close all the curtains and doors, blocking out as much natural light as possible – the darker the better. Finally, turn off the lights and invite someone to read the Bible passage again using a low-powered torch for light. The key words should become highly visible in the darkened room. Take time reflect and to pray.

30. Lifeline

Invite young people to chart their lives to date, pin-pointing significant events on maps you provide. To promote diversity, provide each member with photo-copies of both a world and national map. Using a marker-pen, each young person should mark and date the place of their birth. From there, they should draw a line to – and date – another location that is significant to them. This process should be repeated until their lifeline takes them to the time and place where the small or cell group is meeting. Significant places could include places where they have lived, memorable holidays, family influences, and so on. Invite each member to talk the rest of the group through their lifeline. Use the opportunity to foster conversation.

31. High church

Church architecture may not at first sound particularly enthralling for young people but, with the help of a knowledgeable guide, it can live. Many historic church buildings are crammed full of design, artefacts and win-dows that are rich in symbolism. Arrange to take your group to such a building and, if possible, arrange for someone knowledgeable to be present. Use questions to guide young people's thinking and reflection. What is being depicted in this stained-glass window? What does the layout of this building tell us about the priorities of this church? What aspects of God's nature does this building highlight? Try exposing your young people to different church traditions. If they are used to worshipping God in an historic building try taking them to a 'free church' building with simple design features. However, if this is what they are more familiar with take them instead to a 'high church' building.

32. Scrabble

Obtain a game of *Scrabble* and use it to form the basis of the cell group session.

- *Welcome*: As each member arrives, invite them to register their attendance by spelling out their name on the board using the *Scrabble* letters. Depending on how much time you have available, begin a game of *Scrabble*.

- *Worship*: Invite members to spell out prayers using the *Scrabble* pieces. Read an appropriate Bible passage.

- *Word*: Once you have taken a few minutes to outline the basis of the teaching, invite the group to play a game of *Scrabble*, with double scores given for key words relevant to the session theme. Use the opportunity to ask probing questions that build young people's understanding and awareness.

- *Witness*: Invite members of the group to spell out the names – or initials – of those they are currently praying for. Conclude by praying for each person named.

33. Mystery worshipper

To widen your young people's awareness of the diverse approaches to worship, take them to a series of different church services in your town. The week before, ask the group to agree a set of questions that will form the basis of the assessment. After attending each service, ask the group to use the questions to reflect on what they observed. The following criteria may be helpful:

- Quality of welcome.

- Type of worship.

- Relevance of the message.

- Environmental factors e.g. seating, architecture ...

- Spiritual high.

- Spiritual low.

34. Film critics

Take the group to the cinema to see an age-appropriate film. Alternatively, rent a video. Afterwards, take time to review the film. Use this as an opportunity for conversation and encourage your young people to be aware of the influences – good and bad – that the media often have. What key issues did the film highlight? What aspects of God's character were mirrored by parts of the film? What aspects of the film were challenges to God's nature? What overall rating do you give the film?

35. Video diaries

Invite members of the group to make short video diaries.

36. Bible text

Text messaging, using mobile telephones, is changing both the way we communicate as well as the way we write. The original limitation of just 160 characters or digits per message led to the development of 'text speak'. A national competition challenged people to 'text' the Lord's Prayer using just 160 digits. The winner began HI PA U R IN HVN ... Challenge your group to translate a passage of the Bible into 'text speak'. End by sending the 'text' either to each other or to those outside of the group.

37. Grave matters

Visit a local graveyard and spend time looking at some of the tombstones. Who lived the longest? Who died the youngest? What is the oldest tombstone? What would you like to be written about your life? Be sensitive to young people's varying familiarity with death, particularly if someone has recently experienced bereavement. Also, ensure the group is sensitive to the location and behaves appropriately.

38. Bench-marking

In business, 'bench-marking' is used to compare one industry with another, with the aim of importing new ideas. For example, hospital managers may examine the hotel industry to see how they organise their catering or accommodation. The church can learn much from other service providers. Arrange to take your young people to a new supermarket and ask them to identify lessons that could improve the profile or usefulness of their local congregation.

39. Video montage

Select a Bible passage for the group to reflect upon like, for example, Psalm 139. Ask them to bring to the next group session some video or TV footage that could be incorporated into a short video montage to accompany the reading. At a basic level, it is possible to edit material by connecting two video recorders together. Played back with the TV sound off, the video montage can accompany the reading and/or music from CD or tape player. However, more sophisticated editing is more readily available using home video equipment or computer software. Spending time thinking about which images to use will enable the group to reflect on, and debate, the Bible passage.

40. Group website

Invite the group to design their own website. Be careful not to list personal details that could compromise the safety of group members, including addresses and telephone numbers. Use this as an opportunity to ask the young people probing questions about why they meet and what the purpose of the group is.

41. Labyrinth

One refreshing approach to worship is to create a labyrinth. This takes worshippers on a journey via various stages, each comprising a different spiritual reflection or activity. If the youth ministry comprises more than one small or cell group, invite each group to construct one stage. These might include video montages, statements, artefacts, Bible readings or prayers.

42. Fund-giving

At a time when so much fundraising emphasis is on 'fleecing' others through sponsored events, challenge your young people to learn the art of giving. Suggest to the group that they identify a social cause that they feel committed to. Ask them to find out as much as possible about the organisations that serve in this field. Give them at least a month's notice and then host a fun evening at which they will have plenty of opportunity to give. Remember, God loves cheerful givers! You could auction everything from a meal to a glass of water. You might want to tie this in with a national fundraising event such as Red Nose Day or Children in Need. Following the principle of the 'widow's mite' be careful not to acknowledge just those that give the most money; those who give less may have exercised greater self-sacrifice. How about setting an example by pledging to match from your own resources whatever the group gives.

43. Meeting God

Many young Christians have been brought up to believe the place to meet God is in worship services. The Bible reminds us that we sometimes encounter God, or his angels, when we meet the poor or oppressed (Mt. 25:35, 36; Heb. 13:2). Make contact with a local or national homeless project and arrange an opportunity for your young people to experience first-hand something of its work. Use the opportunity to help the group members recognise the spiritual, as well as social, significance of this work. Afterwards, ask the group members to identify where and when they encountered God on this visit.

44. Trust games

There are a growing number of indoor, as well as out-door, rock-climbing schools that provide an opportunity for young people to gain climbing experience. Arrange for your group to go climbing but make sure both the instructor and school are registered. If in doubt, contact your Local Education Authority for advice. Use this as an opportunity to explore issues of trust, faith and doubt.

45. High points

Set your group the challenge of meeting at the highest point in the neighbourhood. You should all travel together and be able to gain access legally. Examples might include the top of a multi-storey car park, a block of flats or a big hill. Once there, ask your group to tell you what they see. Keep asking them until their answers begin to relate to people. Invite them to suggest approx-imately how many people live in your neighbourhood. What do they believe God thinks about this neighbour-hood? Challenge them to reflect on God's love for all these people, and remind them of the part they can play in mission.

46. Anatomic challenge

Search through your medical contacts to obtain items that display the human anatomy. These might include books, models and charts. If you know a doctor who might be willing to participate in this session, all the bet-ter. Challenge the group to identify or locate various anatomical parts and connect them to other sections of the human body. Read 1 Corinthians 12:12–30. What does it mean to be part of the body of Christ? What is the significance of the differing body parts? What would be the effect on the human body if we only comprised hands, feet or tongues? In using the body analogy, what is Paul trying to communicate to us? How is this small or cell group a small version of the body of Christ? How does it connect with other parts of the body?

47. What would Jesus say to ...

Ask the group to identify a range of well-known and, ideally, controversial figures. These might include politicians, film stars, DJ's and TV presenters. Agree on which personalities will be included. For each session, ask one or two of the young members to have researched information and evidence relating to their personality. Collectively, the group must decide what would Jesus say to him or her. This is an accessible activity for new members, promotes participation and encourages the young people to think for themselves. Remember, Jesus was often far less judgmental than we are today.

48. Pleased to serve

Invite the group to think of creative ways they might be able to serve others. Today it is rare for people to voluntarily do things for others without expecting some form of reward. Jesus calls us to be servants and to go 'the extra mile'. How might the group demonstrate this in their community or church?

49. Jenga prayers

Obtain a game of *Jenga* – the game of building blocks – and use it to form the basis of your cell group session.

- *Welcome*: As each member arrives, give each one a handful of Jenga blocks. When the group is complete play a game of Jenga.

- *Worship*: Read a Bible passage that focuses on the cross of Christ. Invite the group to reflect and pray, using their *Jenga* blocks to form a large wooden cross on the floor.

- *Word*: Select a few key words from the Bible reading. Challenge the group to spell out each word using all their *Jenga* blocks. Try making this into a time-trial. As each word is formed, ask questions that enable the group to say what its relevance is.

- *Witness*: Invite each member to write on *Jenga* blocks the names – or initials – of those known to them who could become future group members. Take a few minutes to pray for each named person.

50. Spin the bottle

Make a list of questions that later may be asked of the small or cell group members. Select questions that reveal something about the person answering them. These should range from trivia questions, such as 'Who was the first person you fancied?' to more probing questions, such as 'If you could have a one-to-one with God what would you say?'. Cut sheets of card into smaller pieces, each the size of a playing card. On each card leave one side blank and on the other write one of the questions. Arrange the group so they are seated on the floor in a circle and in the middle place an empty bottle. Invite a member to spin the bottle. Whoever the bottle points to has to pick a card from the pack and answer the question. To avoid undue embarrassment, provide each member with one 'No Comment' card. This will allow them just one opportunity in the game to abstain from answering a question. Use the game to lead into conversation about some of the answers that are given.

Endnotes

1. Outward Bound Trust, at Loch Eil, near Fort William, in August 1984.
2. C. Handy, *The Age of Unreason*.
3. Charles Handy argues that this process began, not with the computer chip but, with the discontinuous change resulting from the invention of the chimney, which made it possible for one house to support many rooms, *The Age of Unreason*, 11.
4. Tony Campolo, 'Praxis what you preach' *Youthworker* Jounal, Autumn 1993 and reprinted in *The Youthwork Handbook*, Buckeridge (ed.)
5. The 'Waffle Group' was used at Chawn Hill Christian Centre, Stourbridge. Sessions would begin with the group eating syrup waffles. There was also a brass 'waffle' gong that anyone – group members of leaders – could sound if they detected waffle in the group's conversation.
6. Professor Leslie J. Francis and Dr William Kay, *Teenage Religion and Values*. 13,000 secondary pupils aged fourteen and fifteen years were interviewed.
7. See Gunther Krallmann's excellent *Mentoring for Mission*.
8. See Robert Bank's *Paul's Idea of Community*, 41.
9. www.oasistrust.org/passion
10. John Buckeridge, *Youthwork Magazine*, June 1997, 3.
11. Available from Her Majesty's Stationery Office (HMSO), PO Box 276, London SW8 5DT.

[12] The Baptist Union of Great Britain have produced *Safe From Harm*. This is available from Baptist House, PO Box 44, Didcot OX11 8RT. Tel.: 01235 517711 <www.baptist.org.uk>

[13] For an in-depth view of the NOS story, read Roland Howard's sobering book, *The Rise and Fall of the Nine O'Clock Service*.

[14] I am using the young people's definition of 'youth', which seems to end at twenty-one!

[15] Ted Stump and Adam Pisoni, *Student-led Cell Groups*, price $49.95 (plus postage and packing), available only by mail order from High Impact Publishing, PO Box 5003, Glendale, Arizona 853 12-5003, USA; tel: (+001) 602 979 3544; <www.cellgroup.com>

[16] See Charles Handy's *Understanding Organisations*, 171–2.

[17] See Mt. 9:10–15; 12:1; 14:13–21; 15:29–38; 26:17–29; Mk. 2:15, 16; 3:20; 8:1–9a,14–21; Lk. 7:33–50; 10:38–42; 13:24–27; 14:1–24; 19:1–10; 24:13–43; Jn. 2:1–11; 12:1–8; 13:1–17; 21:4–19

[18] In the Catholic Church, congregations confess their sins to the priests. In evangelical churches the minister tells the congregation what their sins are. The media tells the world what some of the minister's sins are.

[19] Examples of Old Testament heroes include Ex. 15:20, 21; Judg. 5:1–31; 1 Kgs. 18:16–46; Jer. 13:1–11; 18:1–12; Ezek. 4; 37:1–14.

[20] Examples include Lk. 8:4–15; 10:25–37 (his storytelling abilities); Jn.15:1–17 (his use of metaphors); Jn. 2:1–11; 13:1–17 (his symbolic role plays).

[21] 'Imagineers' are the people who design Disney theme parks and rides. They are creative blend of engineers and animators.

[22] See for example Marlene D. LeFever's *Learning Styles*.

[23] See Tony Jeffs and Mark K. Smith's *Informal Education: Conversation, Democracy and Learning*, 6.

[24] This idea is developed further in Bo Boshers' challenging *Student Ministry in the Twenty-first Century*.

Bibliography

Arnold, J., The Big Book on Small Groups (Inter-Varsity Press, 1992)

Astin, H., Body and Cell: Making the Transition to Cell Church (Leamington Spa: CPAS, 2002)

Banks, R., Paul's Idea of Community (Carlisle: Paternoster Press, 1980)

Beckham, B., The Two-winged Church will Fly (Houston: Touch Publications, 1995)

Boshers, B., Student Ministry for the Twenty-first Century (Grand Rapids: Zondervan/ Willow Creek, 1997)

Brierley, D., Joined Up: An introduction to youth work and ministry (Carlisle: Authentic/ Youthwork, 2003)

Bunton, P., Cell Groups and House Churches: What History Teaches Us (House to House Publications, 2002)

Campolo, T., 'Praxis what you preach' Youthworker Journal Autumn 1993 and reprinted in The Youthwork Handbook, Buckeridge (ed.) (Kingsway, 1996)

Donahue, B., The Willow Creek Guide to Leading Life-changing Small Groups (Grand Rapids: Zondervan/Willow Creek, 1996)

Donahue, B. and R. Robinson, Building a Church of Small Groups (Grand Rapids: Zondervan/Willow Creek, 2001)

Finnell, D., Life in his Body (Houston: Touch Publications, 1995)

Ford, K., Jesus for a New Generation (London: Hodder and Stoughton, 1996)

Francis, L. and Dr W. Kay, Teenage Religion and Values (Gracewing, 1995)

Handy, C., Understanding Organisations (London: Penguin, 1985)

—The Age of Unreason (London: Arrow Business Books, 1991)

Howard, R., The Rise and Fall of the Nine O'Clock Service (London: Mowbray, an imprint of Cassell plc, 1996)

Jeffs, T. and M.K. Smith, Informal Education: Conversation, Democracy and Learning (Nottingham: Education Now Publishing/YMCA, 1996)

Krallmann, G., Mentoring for Mission (Hong Kong: Jensco, 1992)

LeFever, M.D., Creative Teaching Methods (David C. Cook Publishing, 1985)

—Learning Styles (David C. Cook Publishing, 1995)

Neighbour, R., Where Do We Go From Here? (Houston: Touch Publications, 1990)

Nicholas, R., Good Things Come in Small Groups (Inter-Varsity Press, 1985)

Potter, P., The Challenge of Cell Church (Leamington Spa: CPAS/BrF, 2001)

Prior, D., The Church in the Home (Crowborough: Marshall Pickering, 1983)

Singlehurst, L., Loving the Lost (Eastbourne: Kingsway, 2001)

Snyder, A., The Community of the King (Inter-Varsity Press, 1977)

Stump, T. and A. Pisoni, Student-led Cell Groups (manual) (High Impact Publishing, 1996)

Veernan, D., Small Group Ministry with Youth (Victor Books, 1992)

Ward, P. (ed.), Church and Youth Ministry (Oxford: Lynx, 1995)

—Relational Youth Work (Oxford: Lynx, 1995)

West, L., Cell it: How to Start Youth Cells (Harpenden: Youth With A Mission UK, 1997)

Willard, D., The Connecting Church: Beyond Small Groups to Authentic Community (Grand Rapids: Zondervan, 2001)

Youthwork – the Partnership

Oasis, the Salvation Army, Spring Harvest, Youth For Christ and Youthwork Magazine are working together to equip and resource the Church for effective youth work and ministry.

Youthwork – the Initiatives

1. *Youthwork – the Conference*
- An annual training conference to inspire, network and equip – managed by Spring Harvest.
  www.youthworkconference.co.uk

2. *Youthwork – the Magazine*
- A monthly magazine providing ideas, resources and guidance – managed by CCP.
  www.youthwork.co.uk

3. *Youthwork – the Foundation Course*
- A nine-session/18-hour course for volunteer youth workers – managed by Oasis Youth Action, with support from the Salvation Army.
  www.oasistrust.org/youthworkcourse

4. *Youthwork – the Website*

- A gateway to online resources, community, information and learning – managed by Youthwork Magazine

  www.youthwork.co.uk

5. *Youthwork – the Resources*

- A range of books and materials edited by Danny Brierley and John Buckeridge – managed by Spring Harvest Publishing, an imprint of Authentic Media
  - Going Deeper
  - Developing Practice
  - Resourcing Ministry

Youthwork – the Partners

Oasis Youth Action, the youth division of Oasis Trust, empowers young people and equips youth workers.

Oasis Youth Inclusion tackles social exclusion among young people and children. It offers mentoring, group work and sexual health/relationship education.

Oasis Youth Participation empowers those aged 14 to 25 years

- *Passion* mobilises young people in social action.
- *Frontline Teams* is a UK-based gap year programme (18–25s).
- *Global Action Teams* enable young people to experience life in different countries.

Oasis Youth Work Training equips youth workers and ministers

- *Youthwork – the Foundation Course* is a nine-session/18-hour programme for volunteers.
- *Youth Work Degree* (BA Hons/DipHE) is a professional training programme in youth work and ministry.

To find out more Oasis Youth Action:

Visit: www.OasisTrust.org/YouthAction

Email: YouthAction@OasisTrust.org

Phone: (+44) 20 7450 9044.

Write to: Oasis Youth Action, 115 Southwark Bridge Road, London SE1 0AX, England.

Salvation Army Youth Ministry Unit

The Youth Ministry Unit exists to resource and develop youth work in 1,000 Salvation Army centres around the UK and the Republic of Ireland. It works with the Salvation Army's 18 divisional headquarters to implement local strategies for corps/churches, church plants, youth congregations, social centres and youth inclusion projects. In creating leadership development and mission training programmes for young people, young adults and youth workers, the unit is constantly engaged in developing leaders and missionaries for a twenty-first century Church. In pioneering new projects and programmes, the unit is committed to developing new models of mission. In prioritising the marginalised and the excluded, the unit aims to extend The Salvation Army's rich heritage of social action and social justice. It provides young people with regular opportunities to experience, and engage in, evangelism, worship, discipleship and social action within youth culture. At present the unit is developing a new sub-brand of The Salvation Army focused on young people and young adults. In all this the unit aims to equip, empower and enable young people to reinvent The Salvation Army in their own community, context and culture.

To find out more about the Salvation Army Youth Ministry Unit:

Visit: www.salvationarmy.org.uk

Email: youth@salvationarmy.org.uk

Phone: (+44) 20 8288 1202

Write to: Salvation Army Youth Ministry Unit,
          21 Crown Lane, Morden, Surrey
          SM4 5BY, England.

Spring Harvest

Spring Harvest is an inter-denominational Christian organisation whose vision is to 'equip the Church for action'. Through a range of events, conferences, courses and resources they seek to enable Christians to impact their local communities and the wider world. Spring Harvest Holidays provide an opportunity in France for relaxation and refreshment of body, mind and spirit.

Their Main Event, held every Easter, attracts some 60,000 Christians of all ages, of which over 10,000 are young people. This event also includes specific streams which cater for over 2000 students. Alongside the teaching programme, Spring Harvest provide a range of resources for young people and those that work in youth ministry.

To find out more about Spring Harvest:

    Visit: www.springharvest.org

    Email: info@springharvest.org

    Phone: (+44) 1825 769000

    Write to: Spring Harvest, 14 Horsted Square,
              Uckfield, East Sussex TN22 1QG,
              England.

YFC

YFC, one of the most dynamic Christian organisations, are taking good news relevantly to every young person in Britain. They help tackle the big issues facing young people today. They're going out on the streets, into schools and communities and have changed the lives of countless people throughout the UK.

Their staff, trainees and volunteers currently reach over 50,000 young people each week and have over 50 centres in locations throughout the UK. They also provide creative arts and sports mission teams, a network of registered groups and a strong emphasis on '3 story' evangelism. YFC International works in 120 nations.

To find out more about YFC:

Visit: www.yfc.co.uk
Email: yfc@yfc.co.uk <mailto:yfc@yfc.co.uk>
Phone: (+44) 121 550 8055
Write to: YFC, PO Box 5254, Halesowen,
           West Midlands B63 3DG,
           England.

Youthwork Magazine

Youthwork Magazine is published monthly by CCP Limited. It is Britain's most-widely read magazine resource for equipping and informing Christian youth workers. It provides ideas, resources and guidance for youth ministry. CCP also publish Christianity+Renewal, Christian Marketplace and Enough magazines. CCP is part of the Premier Media Group.

To find out more about Youthwork Magazine:

Visit: www.youthwork.co.uk

Email: youthwork@premier.org.uk

Phone: (+44) 1892 652364

Write to: Youthwork Magazine, CCP Limited,
Broadway House, The Broadway,
Crowborough TN6 1HQ, England.